S0-ARN-593

*PURR*ables

Words of Wisdom from the World of a Cat

Alma Barkman

STARBURST PUBLISHERS

P.O. Box 4123, Lancaster, Pennsylvania 17604

Credits:

Cover art and illustrations by Bill Dussinger.
Fabric design for cover–Kravet Fabrics of Bethpage, Long Island, New York.
Scripture quotations are from the Revised Standard Version, unless otherwise noted.

Author gratefully acknowledges the Steinbach, Manitoba *Carillon,* for running her weekly column in which Sir Purrcival van Mouser made his debut.

We, the Publisher and Author, declare that to the best of our knowledge all material (quoted or not) contained herein is accurate; and we shall not be held liable for the same.

PURRABLES

Copyright ©1993 by Starburst, Inc.
All rights reserved.

This book may not be used or reproduced in any manner, in whole or in part, stored in a retrieval system or transmitted in any form by any means, electronic, mechanical, photocopy, recording, or otherwise, without written permission of the publisher, except as provided by USA copyright law.

First Printing, December 1993

ISBN: 0-914984-53-5
Library of Congress Catalog Number 92-84309

Printed in the United States of America

For the past eighteen years, from our home in the suburbs I have written, among dozens of other things, a weekly humor column. Deathly afraid of not meeting the deadlines, I frequently found myself "cast into the den," groping around for ideas. In lieu of lions as a source of inspiration, I began to focus my attention on the antics of the family cat. Over the years a composite feline character dubbed Sir Purrcival van Mouser began to emerge, and along with him, a growing awareness of truth from a different "*purr*spective." This book containing "words of wisdom from the world of a cat" is the result.

Alma Barkman

Captivated—

One autumn evening when I was nine years old, a big tortoise-shell cat appeared on our doorstep. Absolutely smitten by the feline affection he so lavishly showered upon me, I invited him in and named him Cicero.

His behavior was exemplary, with one major exception. He took the liberty of angling around to my sister's goldfish bowl, where he allegedly hooked out a seafood snack for himself. We came in from play to find him sitting beside the empty bowl, nonchalantly licking his wet paws. Despite the circumstantial evidence, I stoutly maintained his innocence, but my sister claimed he reeked of fish breath. As presiding judge, my mother ruled in Cicero's favor by giving him the benefit of the doubt.

A few months later Cicero disappeared as mysteriously as he had come, and I was to learn firsthand that cats do not belong to anybody.

We belong to them.

It was the first of many lessons taught by Cicero and his successors, for several distinguished members of the van Mouser family have since deigned to grace our household. Believing the world needs more chuckles and less chiding, I write this book of *Purrables* as much for your amusement as for your inspiration.

A merry heart doeth good like a medicine. —Proverbs 17:22 KJV

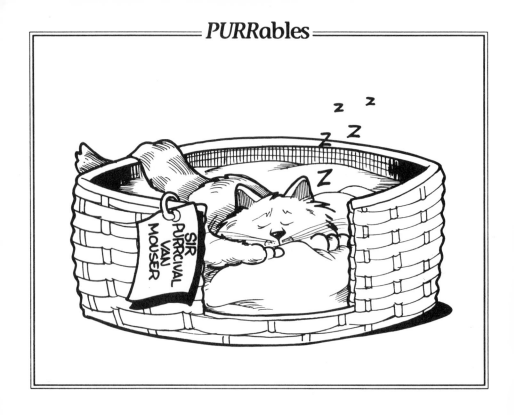

Adopted–

I circle the ad in the pet column of the newspaper: *"Give away to good home. Male kitten, six weeks old."*

He comes wobbling toward me, all eyes and whiskers, four oversized paws supporting a round furry body. His ringed tail punctuates his presence like an exclamation mark. I know at once that this is the very cat we need to carry on the fine old tradition of family pet. We take him home.

But what shall we call him? His demeanor suggests a certain noble ancestry, and he does have a very distinctive purr. So "Sir Purrcival van Mouser" he is–dubbed Purrcival for short.

At first people are quite impressed. They presume a cat with a name of that caliber can only be purchased with money–*lots* of money. When I tell them quite the opposite is true, they begin to scoff. Imagine! Conferring a name like Sir Purrcival van Mouser upon an ordinary alley cat. How preposterous can one get?

Sir Purrcival is not concerned. From his viewpoint, the price one could command as a pedigreed pussycat is not to be compared with the status he enjoys as family pet.

A good name is to be chosen rather than great riches. Favor is better than silver or gold. –Proverbs 22:1

Impulsive—

It doesn't take long for little Sir Purrcival to feel right at home. He does take catnaps, but offhand I can't say just when. If he isn't chasing a fly to the top of the drapes, he's stalking pretend spiders down in the basement.

Today he jumps up on the windowsill and discovers my plants. I doubt the tomato sets will ever progress beyond the three-leaf stage if Purrcival insists on pruning them back so severely. I threaten to reduce him to a bobcat if he doesn't behave, but he takes no notice. Two minutes later he scales my leg like a hydro pole.

The neighborhood varmints and all those pesky dogs had better beware when I turn Sir Purrcival loose. He's a cat who fights fire with spitfire. The resulting chaos will keep the whole canine neighborhood on the defensive for months to come. But it will also keep Sir Purrcival on his tiptoes as well.

He that seeketh mischief, it shall come to him. —Proverbs11:27bKJV

PURRables

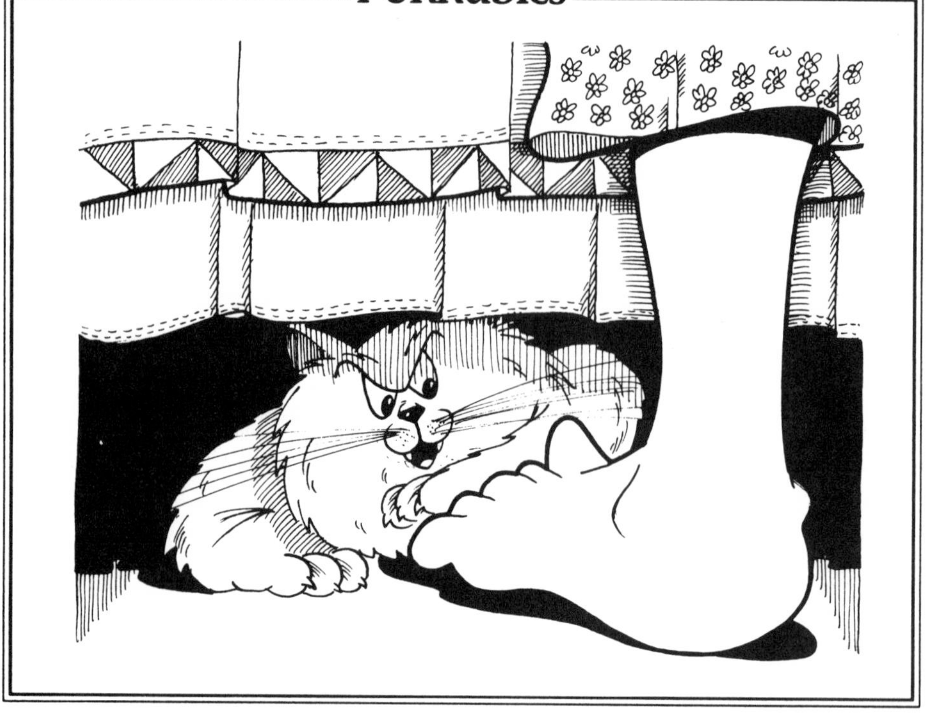

Mischievous—

I am making the final trip down the darkened hall to bed when a phantom object with piercing claws pounces on my back. Little Sir Purrcival has been lying in wait on top of the sofa to lunge at me when I pass.

Now that he has me sufficiently terrorized, he hides under the bed and keeps swiping at my bare feet while I undress. I dare say it is the first time in history that a middle-aged matron has done breakdancing in her nightgown for the benefit of a peeping tomcat.

I collapse into bed, completely exhausted from the unexpected exertion. Things are deathly quiet. There may as well be a Bengal tiger under the bed. I stare into the darkness. I imagine dozens of eyes glinting back at me. My breath comes in short, shallow gasps. Is he still stalking me, even as I lie here?

I close my eyes to ward off the vision.

After what seems an eternity, a wisp of whiskers light as cobwebs brush my face. Little Sir Purrcival has just crept up to say goodnight.

They sleep not, except they have done mischief. —Proverbs 4:16 KJV

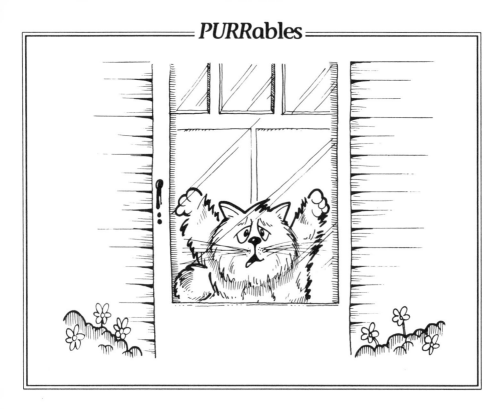

Plaintive—

We retire for the night, but young Purrcival's protests at being left on his own persist long after the accustomed hour. He usually meows a few times and scratches on the bedroom door. When nobody pays attention, he settles down in his basket.

But not tonight. He yowls and meows until our daughter gets up to deal with him, only Purrcival is nowhere in sight. Tracing the sound, she discovers she has accidentally trapped him between the two outside doors when she closed up for the night. He must have been crouching in the shadows on the sill when she latched the storm door. Then, without looking, she quickly locked the inside door, sandwiching him between the two.

Convinced that he has been unjustly condemned to a life of abject misery, and feeling cold, lonely and helpless, young Sir Purrcival is appealing, at the top of his feline lungs, for public sympathy. Deeply moved by his plight, our compassionate daughter does everything in her power to compensate for his misery.

The poor use entreaties. —Proverbs 18:23

Calculating—

Young Sir Purrcival is crouching at the window with tail convulsing, ears flat, eyeballs bulging, whiskers twitching, teeth clacking and claws bared. He must have a bird lined up in the cross hairs of his sights. At his insistence, I snap on his leash and open the door, convinced that no bird in its right mind will ever venture anywhere within killing range.

I am wrong.

Not five minutes later, I go outside and there stands Purrcival with a mouth full of feathers. I stamp my foot threateningly and he lets go of his prey. As it flies away unharmed, Sir Purrcival looks at me defensively, as if to say it's not his fault a stupid bird got caught.

I shorten his leash to curtail his freedom even more. As he sits on the back step in his striped coat behind the bars of the wrought iron railing, he has ample time in which to consider the error of his ways. Indeed, his good behavior during detention convinces me that he will renounce birding in earnest once he is released. Tomorrow he is going to be given an early "*purr*ole."

One who . . . forsakes (transgressions) will obtain mercy. —Proverbs 28:13b

PURRables

Forgiving–

Myron, the neighbor's cat, is not very assertive. The way he pussyfoots around actually raises questions about feline paranoia. Young Sir Purrcival has not yet analyzed him, however, and so the first time Myron cautiously sticks his nose around the corner of the house, Purrcival reacts as he would to any intruder–back arched, ears flat, tail amplified. Poor Myron! He thinks he is suffering delusions and heads for home, with Purrcival in hot pursuit.

Having sufficiently recovered from the trauma of that particular experience, Myron attempts to make a second visit. Creeping ever so circumspectly along the foundation of the house, he edges toward the back door. "Meow?"

Young Sir Purrcival perks up his ears. I open the door just a crack. Myron peeks in politely. Purrcival is not at all sure. *Is this friend or foe?* They touch noses. Purrcival is cautiously inquisitive. After lengthy deliberation they decide they are both Van Mousers, perhaps even long lost relatives. Forsooth!

The two cats have since spent many happy hours together, none of which would have been possible had Myron not *fur*given Purrcival for his unspeakably rude behavior on that very first visit.

One who forgives an affront fosters friendship. –Proverbs 17:9a

PURRables

Opportunistic—

A slow old sausage dog dwells in one of the houses directly behind us. He has a habit of waddling along with his ears over his eyes and his nose to the ground. Today, he looks up just in time to see young Sir Purrcival getting ready to pounce on him.

The pooch is so terror-stricken, instead of taking the steps, he tries to escape by negotiating a shortcut up the *side* of his sun deck.

It isn't the most dignified retreat in history. The dog has such short legs and such a long wheel-base that his undercarriage scrapes in the middle and he just hangs there, helplessly suspended. His hind-quarters are completely vulnerable to the sharp claws of the tomcat, and young Purrcival is wasting no time in taking advantage of the situation. All the poor old pooch can do is whine for mercy while I run to rescue him.

Sir Purrcival is *purr*plexed. As naive and immature as he is, he sees no reason why I should intervene in any of these daring little exploits. From his limited experience, big black cats run away and long fat dogs are sissies—so why be cautious?

Discretion will guard you, understanding will watch over you. —Proverbs 2:11 NASB

PURRables

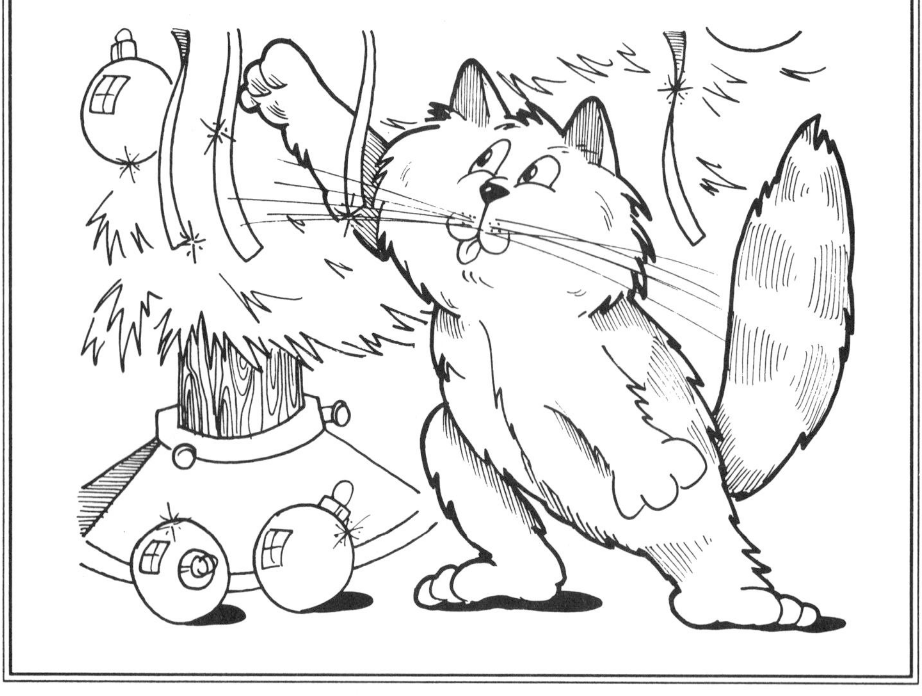

Greedy—

Young Purrcival tries to eat the tinsel off the lowest branches of the Christmas tree as fast as we decorate it.

"If that cat swallows any more of that stuff, he's gonna die from an acute case of *tin*selitis," warns friend hubby. But Purrcival seems nowhere near expiring, even though the tinsel continues to disappear.

And then early one morning he throws up on the kitchen floor. My first reaction is, *Oh, oh, this could be the beginning of the end. Looks like he's been bleeding internally from the tinsel.*

On second thought, he is tearing up and down the hall at top speed, not exactly symptomatic of a *purr*forated ulcer.

And then I discover the source of his nausea. In the rush to get ready for school, the teenager has forgotten to finish a partial slice of toast spread thickly with raspberry jam, and Purrcival has deviously indulged. It was good while it lasted, but those annoying little raspberry seeds tend to stick between his teeth, and trying to dislodge them is like chewing stones.

Bread gained by deceit is sweet, but afterward the mouth will be full of gravel. —Proverbs 20:17

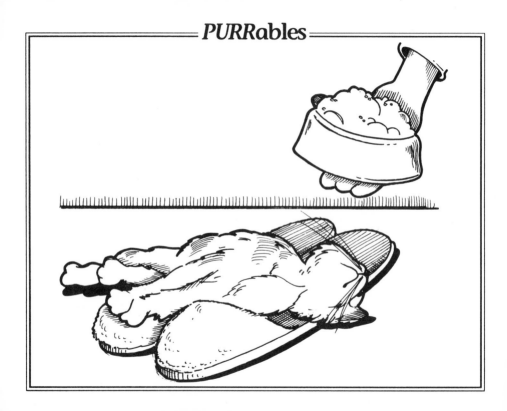

Fickle—

Sir Purrcival has such a vigorous appetite I decide to take advantage of it to teach him a trick. Whenever hunger pangs strike, he goes straight to his dish. I tell him to "lie down and die;" then he flops over in a dead faint, or the feline equivalent thereof.

Discovering the trick pays such satisfying dividends to his stomach, he has today exhausted all of his proverbial nine lives and it isn't even noon yet. Without so much as a word of encouragement, he has "died" in front of his dish, in the middle of the kitchen floor, on top of my slippers, and at half a dozen other locations where I do not expect to trip over a dead cat. It gets my attention every time.

I try to convince myself that Purrcival would be just as obliging even without the rewards I give him. Much to my chagrin, I soon discover that he is a fickle friend, not at all selective in choosing the people for whom he is willing to "die." Since all he really forfeits is a measure of feline dignity in return for a substantial reward, he is ready and waiting to make his pseudo sacrifice for any number of people. If the truth were known, any number of cats, if similarly bribed, would probably perform the same trick.

Many seek the favor of the generous, and everyone is a friend to a giver of gifts. —Proverbs 19:6

Resourceful—

In a move born of desperation, Sir Purrcival has lowered himself to a bit of ingenuity.

He has invented a new doorbell. Teetering up on the wrought-iron railing, he braces himself against the house with one front foot, then plucks at the screen door with his claws.

The first day he tested out his little experiment, I thought there was a burglar prying loose the screen door. With fearful heart I crept around the corner, dreading the thought of catching a thief red-handed.

There was nobody there.

Well, that's not *exactly* true. How dare I call Sir Purrcival van Mouser a *nobody?* He with the lofty bearing and snobbish nose? Indeed! When I opened the door he strolled in like the aristo*cat* he is, the only sign of his inner contempt being a haughty jerk of his tail.

So now at the end of his daily constitutional, he knows how to attract my attention, playing his makeshift harp and yowling at the top of his lungs. Granted, it is not the most dignified pose for a proud cat to assume, but it does have its unexpected dividends. Not only does the door swing open promptly, but Sir Purrcival is welcomed and stroked and praised for being the intelligent cat he has just proven himself to be.

At the entrance of the doors (wisdom) cries out. —Proverbs 8:3 NASB

Satisfying—

When Purrcival comes strolling across the grass with a young robin hooked on one fang, I grab him by the tail and hang on. When he opens his mouth to vehemently protest my interference, the bird gets free.

Banishing Sir Purrcival to the basement, I call our teenaged son and hand him the garden fork. "I have to leave right away for a meeting, but go dig some earthworms, chop them up and feed that baby robin."

He pales considerably. "Did you say. . . chop . . . them . . . up?"

"Be glad you don't have to chew them first!" I add by way of encouragement.

When I return two hours later, Purrcival is still decrying the loss of his prey. "That tomcat oughta be clobbered!" declares our son.

As for the baby robin, after several mouthfuls of worm nuggets, its strength was greatly reinforced. Hearing its orphaned pleas, Mama Robin flew back to take over feeding duties from our son.

He can hardly believe that he actually saved a life just by digging worms. "Such a little thing to do for such a great sense of satisfaction."

Those who are kind reward themselves. –Proverbs 11:17

Exploratory—

Sir Purrcival is scouting around the house for ways and means to enrich his life style. Assaying every possibility, with the intensity of a prospector out panning for gold, he chances to look under the frig. *Eureka!*

He immediately stakes claim to the territory, lying flat across the kitchen floor to get a better look. Whatever he sees, you would think he had struck a fortune. With one paw he reaches underneath the frig as far as he possibly can; but all he manages to unearth is a dust ball. *Achoo!* He shakes the fuzzies off his whiskers. But there is still a veritable bonanza waiting to be retrieved. Hopelessly smitten with goldrush fever, he reaches way underneath with the other paw. More fuzzies. *Gesundheit!*

It's a ticklish business, but the pile of pay dirt finally yields four marbles, a safety pin, two pencils and a pine cone. *A pine cone! Forsooth!* To a tomcat, such a nugget is practically priceless. Examine it, carry it, hide it, seek it, search for it, chase it, cherish it—a more precious treasure the tomcat could not imagine. And to think it was buried under the frig all this time, waiting to be discovered.

. . . search for (wisdom) as for hidden treasures. —Proverbs 2:4

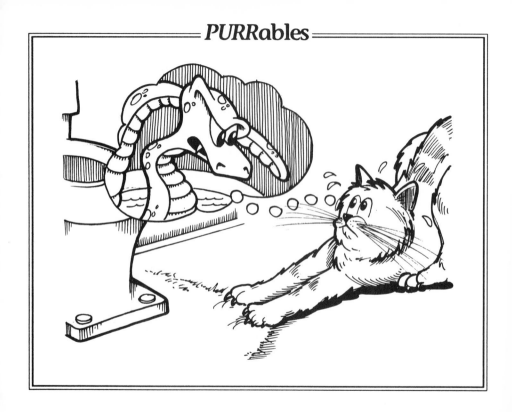

Dubious—

I recoil in horror when I read that a pet snake can escape down the toilet, swim through the plumbing and surface in a neighbor's toilet. If that ever happens to me, I will die of a heart attack and topple off the throne.

Today I wonder if my time has come. Sir Purrcival and I are in the den across from the bathroom and suddenly the water in the toilet bowl gurgles mysteriously. The hair rises along Sir Purrcival's back and cold chills go down my own spine.

We both edge closer to the toilet. Could it be a snake surfacing? The water gurgles again, and Sir Purrcival takes no chances. He skids across the floor and jumps up onto my filing cabinet. I appeal for friend hubby to come to our rescue. "And bring a big brick to put on the toilet lid."

Friend hubby reassures me that the strange noises I have been hearing are probably caused by city employees cleaning out the local sewer line. I believe him, simply because I so desperately *want* to—not because I am convinced.

But Sir Purrcival remains dubious. To be on the safe side, he carefully avoids walking anywhere near the toilet, just in case a big boa constrictor actually *does* surface.

The simple believe everything, but the clever consider their steps. –Proverbs 14:15

PURRables

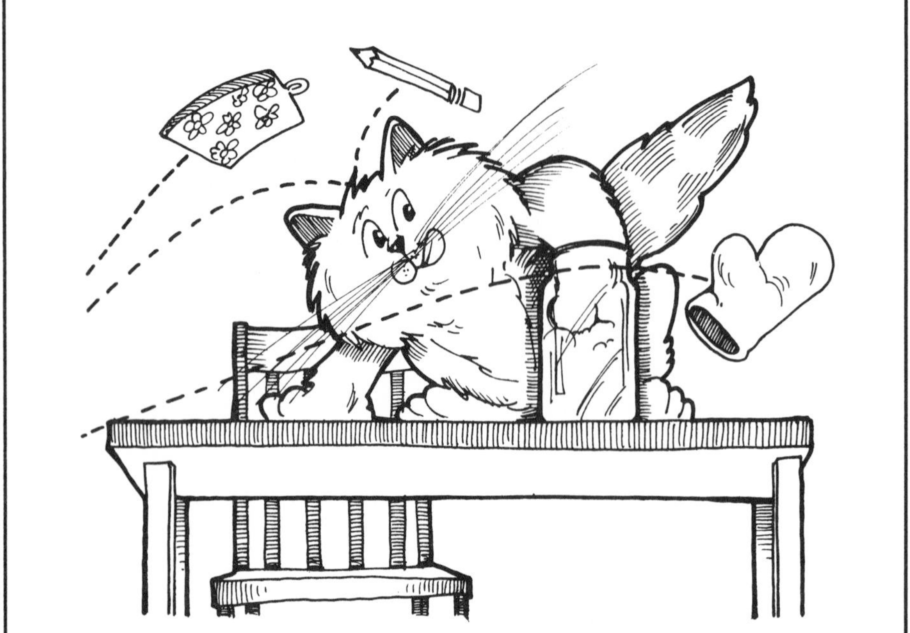

Tempted—

When his own dish sits empty for what Sir Purrcival considers a prolonged length of time, he seems to think his only recourse is to steal leftovers. As I talk on the phone, I see such intentions materializing. But I can hardly terminate a business call by using the excuse the tomcat is swiping a sausage from my kitchen table. The party on the other end of the line would no doubt be properly horrified. Besides, it isn't exactly true. Sir Purrcival is not stealing any meat. What really captures his fancy is the coffee whitener, only the neck of the jar is too narrow.

I underestimate his ingenuity. After sniffing the contents, Purrcival thoroughly licks his paw, sticks it into the open jar of coffee whitener and licks his paw clean. Not once, but several times. Lick, dip, lick . . . .

Still trying to sensibly uphold my end of the phone conversation, I keep stamping my feet and pelting the tomcat with a steady barrage of oven mitts, pot holders, pens, pencils, tea towels, erasers and any other ammunition within reach. He takes no notice whatsoever.

When Sir Purrcival thinks circumstances justify it, questions of ownership and ethics simply slide off his back.

Feed me with food convenient for me, lest I . . . steal. —Proverbs 30:8,9 KJV

*PURR*ables

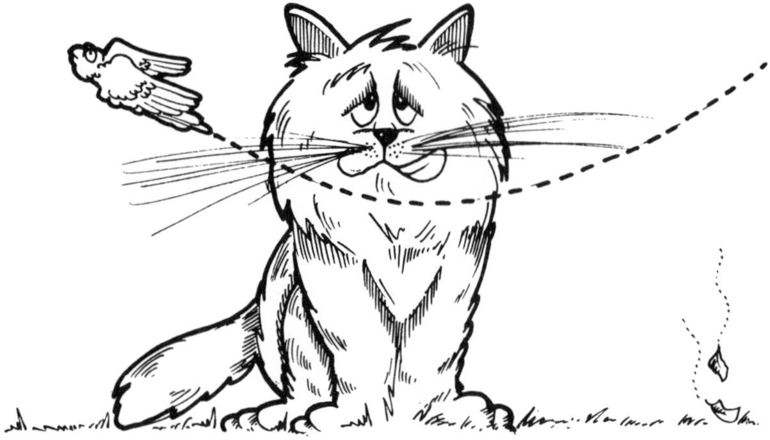

Deceitful—

On numerous occasions I have watched Sir Purrcival try to catch a robin, only to have it fly away right under his nose. Not willing to concede a loss, he tries to salvage his pride. First he sits down right on the spot and vigorously licks his lips; after which he washes all imaginary traces of feather from his face. It is his way of trying to provoke the neighbor's dog to jealousy by implying that he has just indulged in bird, and "Sorry about you, old boy."

Cats are like that. They have no scruples whatever about lying.

In late autumn a flock of small yellowish birds land in the garden patch, and if I do say so myself, I have never seen birds with fewer brains. Using a left hook, Sir Purrcival literally plucks them right out of the air as they swoop in low to the ground. The yard can be literally strewn with the remains of the unwary, but if I scold Purrcival for his "fowl" deeds, he just sits and licks his lips as if to say "Birds? What birds? I don't see any birds, do you?"

Unfortunately, no. He has just decimated the flock and the survivors have fled for their own safety.

Lying lips conceal hatred. —Proverbs 10:18

Defensive—

Sir Purrcival enjoys lolling under the maple trees in our front yard. Stretched out luxuriantly in the shade, with the hint of a smile spread across his furry face, he gives the distinct impression of "feline fine."

It drives dogs crazy.

Any pooch that happens to be trotting down the road at the end of a leash cannot help but see this big fat cat dozing there in the grass. The canine instinct to give chase immediately switches into overdrive. An inattentive jogger out exercising her pooch may suddenly find herself being pulled right down through the ditch and up the other side at breakneck speed.

As the aggressive mutt approaches, there is a slight flexing of the claws, a glint of indignation in the eyes, but Sir Purrcival maintains his dignity. After all, this yard is *his* domain, these people *his* pride, and no hyena on the end of a leash is going to usurp his *terror*tory. What possesses some common cur to even issue such a challenge? Nose-to-nose with His Royal Highness, the dog suddenly wonders the exact same thing, and hurries off in urgent need of a fire hydrant.

Sir Purrcival remains as undisputed king of the jungle.

The righteous are as bold as a lion. —Proverbs 28:1

PURRables

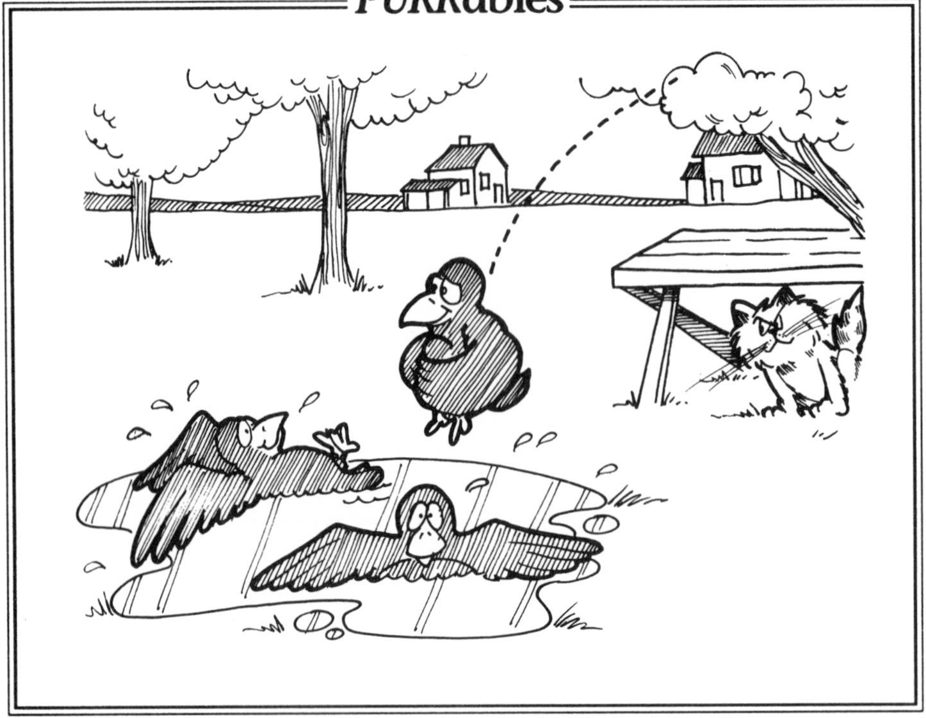

Contemptuous—

A family of crows has just hatched in a tree next door.

Now be it understood that Sir Purrcival is quite capable of vanquishing most members of the bird species. He frequently proves his prowess by coming home with the remains of a sparrow impaled on his fangs.

But these crows are a wicked lot. And *big!* Their wingspread is enough to darken the sun when they sweep in low over Sir Purrcival. He winces perceptibly at the very *thought* of being mistaken for cat carrion. As if to add insult to imaginary injury, when Purrcival falls asleep under the picnic table, a curious young crow actually sneaks up and delivers a tentative peck to his pelt.

Stupid vulture! Can't even tell the difference between a sleeping tomcat and a recent roadkill!

From that point on, Sir Purrcival's testiness toward crows in general knows no bounds. Just the noise they make is enough cause for anxiety, and those black-curved beaks are an absolute menace to a feline who treasures his shiny green eyes. When the whole raucous family swoops down for a bath in a nearby puddle, Sir Purrcival is downright contemptuous, convinced more than ever that crows are nothing but "raven maniacs."

When wickedness comes, contempt comes also. —Proverbs 18:3

PURRables

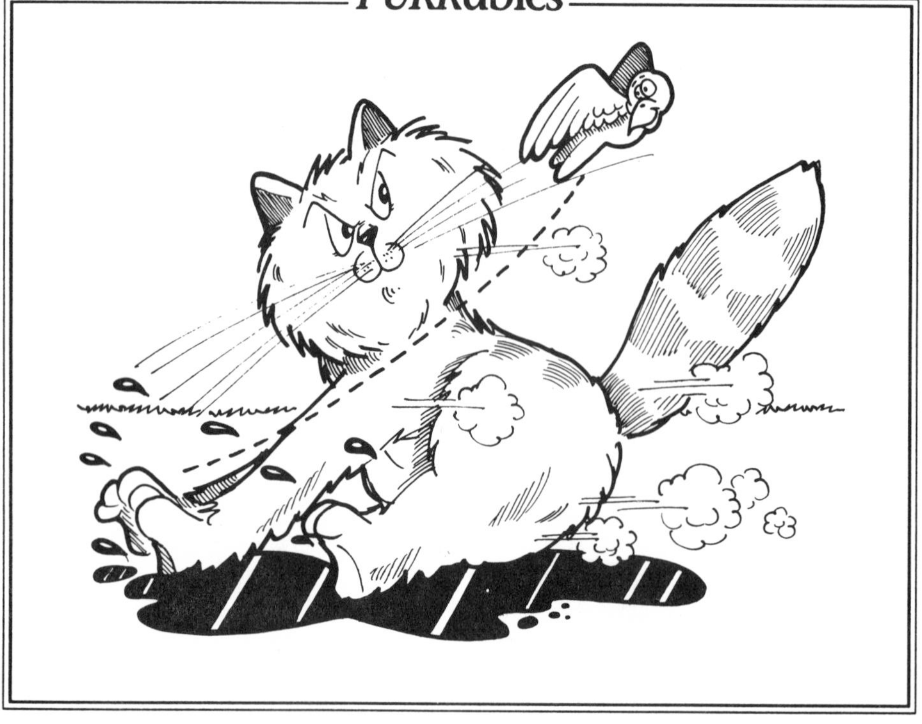

Self-Condemned—

Every time it rains, a big mud puddle forms at the end of our driveway, creating a natural bird bath. Before long the robins strut right in and fluff out their feathers, immediately assuming proportions twice their normal size.

The temptation is too much for the tomcat, who concludes that a bird self-basted with water *has* to be juicier than a plain dry one. He pounces out from behind the spirea bushes and the robins take to the air like a squadron of vertical lift-off jets. Squinting after them, the tomcat licks his lips in exasperation. Not only have the birds escaped his clutches, he has skidded to a stop in the slimy ooze at the edge of the puddle.

Flicking the mud from alternate paws, he comes hobbling up the driveway and slumps down on the back step, a prisoner of his own dark thoughts. Unable to ignore the strong feline instinct for cleanliness, Purrcival's muddy feet have sentenced him to solitary confinement as effectively as if he were shackled to a ball and chain. Sitting behind the bars of the wrought iron railing, he licks his paws and glares in anger at those annoying robins cheerfully celebrating their freedom in a nearby tree.

In the transgression of evil there is a snare, but the righteous sing and rejoice. —Proverbs 29:6

PURRables

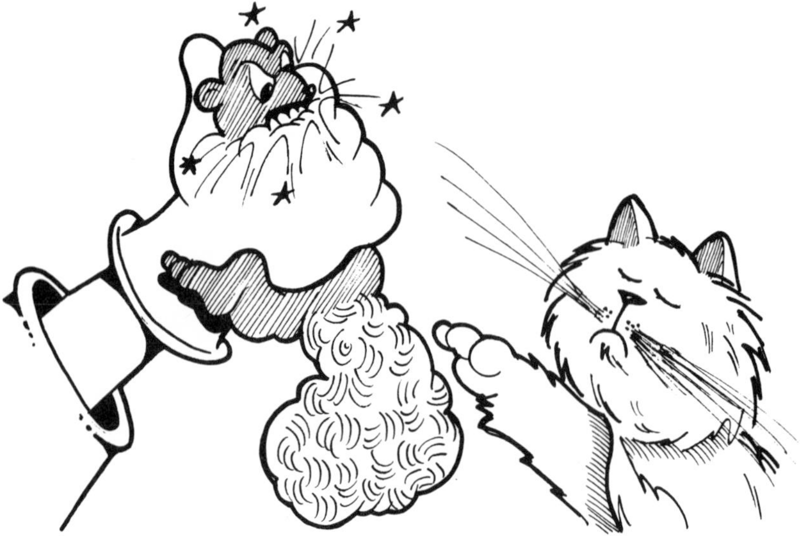

Offended—

This morning I notice a tired young gray squirrel being stalked across the grass by one curious tomcat, who corners him under some bushes at the back step. Sir Purrcival is *furious* when I intervene. To his way of thinking, no self-respecting tomcat should *ever* have to suffer the indignity of being locked in the basement while one of those saucy whippersnappers roams free.

Grabbing an old pair of mittens, I manage to pick up the exhausted young squirrel, with the intention of returning him to his nest in the old shed. He is not particularly grateful, sinking razor-sharp teeth into my fingers while I carry him across the yard. As I open the door to the shed, I can see Mama Squirrel anxiously waiting to welcome her prodigal boy back to the fold.

As for Sir Purrcival, he sniffs at my bleeding fingers with utter disdain, highly indignant that one of those ungrateful, irresponsible squirrels should merit any attention whatsoever. Do they not just fritter away the seasons, while he serves as chief mouser of this household year after year? Sir Purrcival is offended beyond words. Spurning all efforts to console him, he promptly turns on his heels and struts straight through the door in search of recognition elsewhere.

Wrath is cruel, anger is overwhelming, but who is able to stand before jealousy? —Proverbs 27:4

Spared–

The family of gray squirrels born and raised in the tool shed take to the trees today, raining down acorns like hailstones. No matter how he tries, Sir Purrcival can't stop the plague.

At first he figures he can frighten the squirrels into submission by being the highly visible foe. Then, he struts out to the middle of the garden plot and licks his lips in a very menacing fashion.

The squirrels pay no attention. None whatsoever!

Sir Purrcival is highly offended. Can they not see his long sharp fangs stained with the blood of countless kills? Do they not tremble in their squirrel suits at the very thought of being the next victims?

Not on your life! Those squirrels are having too much fun up in the trees to entertain any ideas of immediate extinction. And besides, any fat old tomcat plumped down in the middle of the garden is probably as lazy as he looks. Or is he? One of the squirrels inches closer and closer, all on the pretext of gathering nuts.

Sir Purrcival waits with bated breath. Let that squirrel come just one acorn closer and . . . POUNCE! The tomcat gives a mighty spring.

The squirrel? It scampers back the way it came, across the grass, along the fence and up the tree to safety.

Those who guard their way preserve their lives. –Proverbs 16:17b

Betrayed—

Sir Purrcival has concluded that the only way to subdue those fleet-footed squirrels is to ambush them from behind the raspberry canes. Wait until they make a run for it and cut 'em off at the pass.

His plan may work, but in his eagerness Sir Purrcival forgets to notify his tail. There he is, squatted flat to the ground, his coat camouflaged against the foliage, his ears flat, his claws bared, every muscle taut, but his tail is flapping back and forth like a red flag in a danger zone.

The squirrels all take heed and run the other way.

In sullen fury, the tomcat comes slinking back to the house, pausing now and then to look back at what might have been the site of the greatest squirrel massacre in history—had he not been betrayed by his tail. Worse yet, nothing short of disaster will ever separate him from the source of his problem. That old traitor-tail will dog him all the days of his life, and he will have to groom it and guard it and generally treat it like the unruly villain it is.

I empathize with Sir Purrcival's frustration, because his tail, like a gossip's tongue, can never be trusted to keep a secret. At an inopportune moment it will give away all it knows, or even anticipates. And sometimes what it only imagines.

He who goes about as a talebearer reveals secrets. —Proverbs 11:13 NASB

Indolent—

Like a siren approaching the emergency entrance, we hear Sir Purrcival's mournful yowls growing louder and louder. It's our signal to swing into action. The milk is poured, cat yummies rattle into the bowl, and the door opens. In hobbles Sir Purrcival van Mouser, suffering an acute case of feline self-pity.

It has been such a long cold night; his whiskers are stiff as broom straws and he needs the warmest bed in the house in order to bring his temperature back to normal. But first he must replenish his loss of calcium with a good stout drink of milk; otherwise the old caudal appendage is apt to stay permanently limp. His stomach ulcers having healed after that last bout with the neighbor's dog. He can even tolerate solid cat food. Now to stretch out for a long recuperative rest, far away from nagging screech owls and other nocturnal distractions.

Purrcival is still sleeping, long after other Van Mousers have diligently prowled through neighborhood yards in search of those tasty morsels typical felines love to catch. Not Sir Purrcival. He would much rather slumber away the hours on a soft bed, completely confident that he is one cat who should never have to work for a living.

Laziness casts into a deep sleep. —Proverbs 19:15a NASB

Sly—

My tomcat has been gone for nearly two weeks. I know, I know. People keep telling me it's the season a young man's fancy turns, etc. My tomcat is not that young. In years, maybe, but experience has aged him considerably. He has always been inclined to meet life head-on, and his face bears the scars to prove it. Claw marks crisscross his nose, his ears are chewed lacy and his hide shows evidence of numerous old battle wounds.

You may be thinking I haven't lost much, but as my neighbor always says when she sees Sir Purrcival out in the yard, "Now there's a tomcat with character." He returns the compliment by deigning to sit on her doorstep as a conversation piece when she has company. Actually, he is not just sitting over there flattering her visitors with his great green eyes for no reason. He is sizing up her bird population from close range.

And that's exactly where I find him this morning. He is lolling in the sunshine on her back step, wearing that "ask me no questions, I'll tell you no lies" expression. I solemnly warn him that he is not to run away again, but he just blinks at me lazily, as if he is already formulating ideas for his next rendezvous.

One who winks the eyes plans perverse things. —Proverbs 16:30

Impetuous—

The tomcat has been very edgy of late. He seems to think he is living in a haunted mansion and all sorts of weird sounds keep getting on his nerves. Release the plug in the bathtub and the sound of water gurgling down the drain annoys him. Turn up the thermostat and the currents of warm air rub his fur the wrong way. When he tries to get some shuteye, those miserable birds create too much racket at the feeder.

Today he tackles the squeak in the kitchen floor. I can tell by his eyes he is getting riled-up, but at his age I never expect him to go to such lengths—pouncing and scratching and carrying on like a veritable tiger. Fearing for the welfare of my floor, I try to offset potential claw damage by tiptoeing around the troublesome spot.

Gone but not *fur*gotten. Whenever I inadvertently step in the wrong place and trigger off the offending squeak, Purrcival is right there to do serious battle with it all over again. He comes tearing down the hall angrily intent on eradicating that elusive noise once-and-for-all. And then when we laugh at his antics, he finds himself the humiliated victim of his own rash actions.

One who has a hasty temper exalts folly. —Proverbs 14:29

PURRables

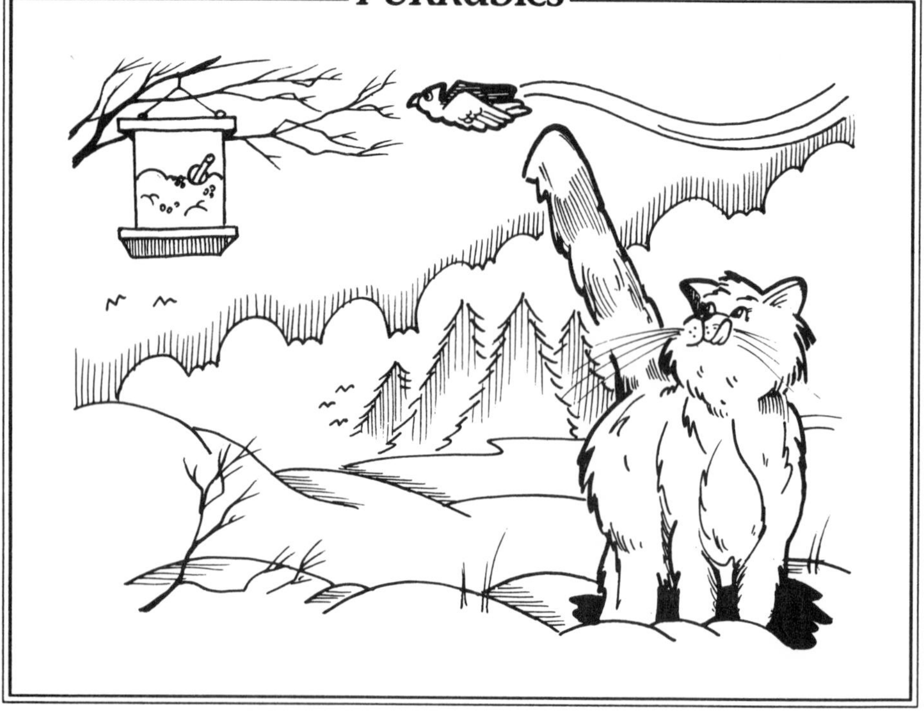

Contradictory—

Sir Purrcival has been pondering why the number of visitors to the bird-feeder has mysteriously declined this past winter.

His idea of big game is a raucous bluejay, the likes of which were once very common in these parts. The tomcat sits in the sunlight for hours, contemplating their demise. Was it a question of depleted bird seed? Cyclical disease? *Overkill?*

Sir Purrcival finds that last one hard to swallow. He is, after all, only *one* tomcat, and the trophy-sized bluejays that hang in his memory are not *that* numerous.

No, judging by his cantankerous attitude toward them, he tends to blame those pesky sparrows. If they didn't gobble up everything in sight, there *would* be more bluejays abounding.

Totally ignoring my admonitions about the folly of blaming others for his own foul deeds, Sir Purrcival persists in taking matters into his own paws. A few minutes later I catch him ambushing another innocent little sparrow from behind a snowbank. When sharply scolded, Sir Purrcival just stares at me with unrepentant gaze.

A scoffer does not listen to rebuke. —Proverbs 13:1b

PURRables

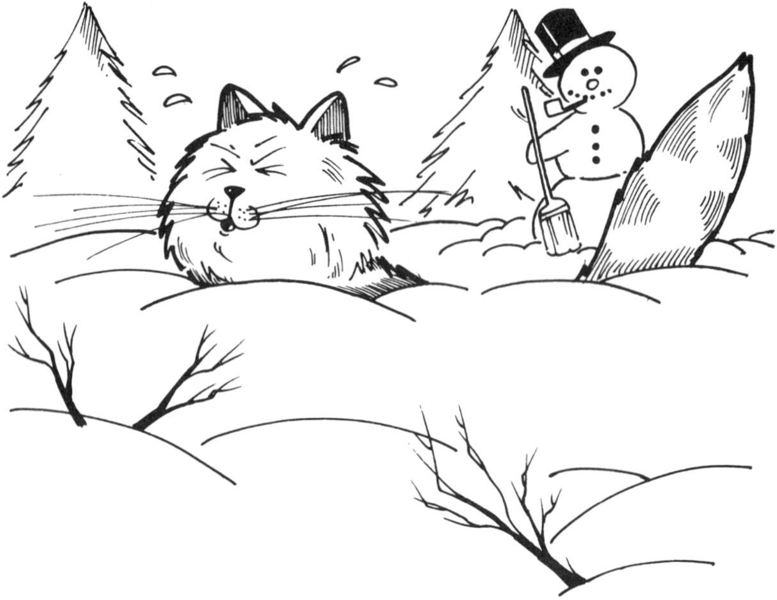

Unpredictable—

When Sir Purrcival hears a familiar voice calling him for lunch, he does not hesitate, especially in winter. He takes whatever shortcuts he can across the deep snowdrifts in our back yard. But today a sudden chinook wind has brought warm weather, only Purrcival does not realize the changing conditions of the snow. I call him for lunch and he takes off across the snowdrifts as usual.

His initial burst of speed keeps him afloat for a time; but then the softened snow gives way beneath his weight and his body starts to sink below the surface. A few desperate plunges and he comes to a full stop, stuck in a snow drift. With nothing showing but his head and his tail, he is yowling for someone to come to his aid.

Like a game warden whose duty it is to save endangered wildlife, I wend my way through the deep drifts of snow. By now I expect Sir Purrcival will be so weak and debilitated from his ordeal that he will not put up much of a struggle.

But felines under stress are unpredictable. As I stoop to pick him up out of the snowbank into which he has sunk, the pain of his wounded ego suddenly turns him into a writhing, snarling, growling bundle of raw nerves. I must be careful indeed to avoid the brutality of his outstretched claws.

Better to meet a . . . bear. . . than confront a fool immersed in folly. —Proverbs 17:12

Whimsical—

When Sir Purrcival leans into the curve as he veers around the corner, unsuspecting visitors had better beware. He may barrel between their legs without losing an ounce of momentum. Then it's across the coffee table and up onto the back of the sofa, at which point he is magically transformed from a fuzzy blur of speed to a prim pussycat, calmly grooming his coat.

A coy cat demurely fixing his fur needs no valid reason for changing back into a demon in disguise. If the fancy strikes, he's off again, propelled by some mysterious fuel not yet discovered by the more indolent species.

Sir Purrcival is that changeable. One minute he is all predator, pursuing some imaginary prey at full speed, a deep, quizzical intensity in his black eyes. Seconds later, he is sitting and staring off into space with vacant expression, his eyes like two lucid marbles, his lethal claws cleverly concealed beneath innocent-looking paws.

Sudden bouts of feline mania, tempered by moments of pure melancholy, are impossible for mere mortals to understand. Any attempts to do so are simply met with haughty disdain, strongly suggesting that Sir Purrcival is safer left alone when he is moody.

Meddle not with them that are given to change. —Proverbs 24:21 KJV

Deluded—

The scowl on Sir Purrcival's face as he strolls in after a night's mousing indicates he has not brought down any big game. When he goes straight to his dish and gobbles down every last morsel, my suspicions are confirmed.

Any other morning he would be satisfied to crawl into his favorite chair and catch up on a long overdue catnap. But not today. When the passions of a big game hunter are aroused, nothing short of a trophy-sized specimen will satisfy the urge. Sir Purrcival is certain he can flush something out from under the sofa. No luck. What about the bed? Only a few dustballs. Maybe downwind in the basement?

A few minutes later he creeps upstairs, and then I hear him signal. His squeaky appeals mean but one thing—the presence of wildlife behind the curtains. I circle around to find him perched on the arm of the easy chair, his gaze fixed to a spot on the window glass. If I will just open the drapes, he will have perfect aim at the biggest bug he has ever stalked.

There is but one problem.

It isn't a bug he sees at all.

It's a drop of dried paint on the windowpane.

Do not rely on your own insight. —Proverbs 3:5b

PURRables

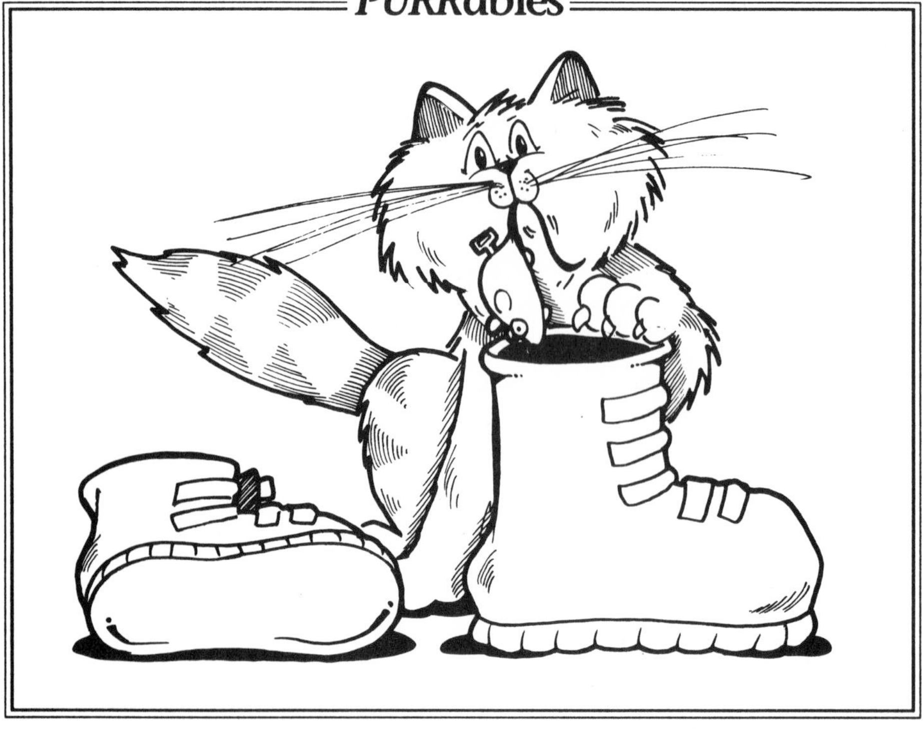

Foolish—

The tomcat is having troubles with a toy mouse. In surly mood, he attacks it viciously, determined to dispose of the pest once and for all. Having inflicted what he deems to be necessary measures, he walks away, an impudent switch of his tail indicating victory at last.

But what's this? He wakes up from his customary catnap, only to discover that the toy mouse is still very much present. Hadn't he just dealt with the varmint minutes ago? Of a truth, a more *purr*sistent mouse he has never encountered in all of his nine lives.

After due and careful consideration, Purrcival picks up the mouse and carries it off to hide in some mysterious corner. *Out of sight, out of mind* seems to be his feline philosophy.

But life occasionally gets dull, with nothing to amuse him. If the toy mouse doesn't show up of its own accord, Purrcival goes to seek it out, looking under beds, in dark closets, under mats. When he finds the mouse exactly where he left it, in somebody's winter boot, he feigns surprise at his discovery. "Imagine meeting you here!"

And then he starts the routine all over again.

A fool reverts to his folly. —Proverbs 26:11

Aggressive—

Sir Purrcival patrols the yard like a proud vigilante, practicing his guerilla tactics on intruding birds and combating the insurgence of field mice. He launches campaigns against butterflies in the flower beds, and lays siege to grasshoppers hiding out among the cucumber vines. Totally disregarding dangerous raspberry thorns, he turns back, singlehandedly, a flock of robins advancing on ripe berries. And should an enemy feline actually infiltrate Sir Purrcival's territory, he declares all out war.

This morning he marches home from hostilities wearing a foe's claw pinned to his chest like a medal of honor. Fearing he may develop an infection, I wait until he is deeply settled into a catnap before approaching him with my tweezers. As I extract the imbedded claw and dress his wound, he growls viciously in his sleep, but I am not about to be deterred. If Sir Purrcival wages senseless wars, he can expect to suffer the pain of battle scars.

Thorns and snares are in the way of the perverse; the cautious will keep far from them. —Proverbs 22:5

Demanding—

As a member of the local union of mousers, Sir Purrcival has a grievance. The price of his favorite cat food has escalated, and at the risk of undermining *purr*duction, management has brought in a cheaper variety. Sir Purrcival deems it a serious rollback.

At first he tries to wheedle me into negotiations by rubbing against my legs at feeding time, gently conceding that *everybody* makes a mistake sometime. When I refuse to yield, he sniffs with disdain and walks away from the bargaining table.

At supper time he establishes a picket line, defying us to cross it in order to reach the supper table. By morning he is becoming very vocal in his demands, tramping back and forth to his dish in a one-cat protest march. He quickly solicits the support of our two teenagers, both of whom make passionate pleas on his behalf. However, neither is willing to assume the extra financial burden posed by the expensive cat food Sir Purrcival is demanding.

As a last resort, the tomcat has staged a hunger strike. His dish is full, his saucer of milk is beside it; but just as a matter of *purr*inciple, he steadfastly refuses to eat.

Such is the end of all who are greedy for gain; it takes away the life of its possessors. —Proverbs 1:19

Secretive—

On the pretext of admiring the blooms, Sir Purrcival furtively visits the neighbor's flower bed in response to the call of nature. And there, with sombre expression, he sits gazing out from among the star-faced petunias.

In order to reach the camouflaged luxury of the flower bed, Purrcival has to go down our back steps, through the carport, across the lane, along the row of willows, up a tree, and down onto a fencepost. From there, if no one is looking, he jumps into the petunia patch. Such effort, and a litter box right within the privacy of his own basement!

The day comes when our neighbor happens to notice that one of her petunias has mysteriously grown whiskers. As she stoops to have a closer look, she calls me to come and see this phenomenon. Afraid she may be highly indignant, I peer cautiously over the fence, and am surprised to see her chuckling over Sir Purrcival, who is making self-conscious use of her flowery facilities. When I confess that it is not the first time he has taken such liberties, she just shrugs. "So who's worried? The petunias are certainly flourishing."

Those with good sense are slow to anger, and it is their glory to overlook an offense. —Proverbs 19:11

Slothful—

Purrcival likes to indulge in birdwatching. And what birds there are to watch! Great bulging robins, meaty flickers, tasty sparrows, dainty ovenbirds, delectable bluejays. Purrcival watches them through the picture window, salivating at the very thought of nabbing one for supper.

But that would mean *work,* and some days Sir Purrcival is just not up to all the extra effort one has to expend in preparing a tasty supper. Just the exertion of licking his lips is rather exhausting today, so he curls his tail around his nose and drifts off to sleep.

Recognizing their chance, the robins descend upon the lawn in droves. With feet braced, tails spread, heads cocked sideways, eyes concentrated, they pull countless earthworms from the damp soil. Stretched to the limit, an occasional worm snaps in half like an elastic band, nearly giving a robin whiplash. But no matter. While the tomcat only *dreams* of a full stomach, the robins enjoy a veritable feast.

The appetite of the lazy craves and gets nothing, while the appetite of the diligent is richly supplied. —Proverbs 13:4

Discerning—

Occasionally, a relaxed yawn disturbs Sir Purrcival's catnap. But as soon as his whiskers fall back into position he is off again to dreamland. He is not easily wakened by such trivia as vacuum cleaners that threaten to suck up his tail, nor doorbells that pound on his eardrums, nor telephones that jangle his nerves. But let a *dog* bark in the distance, and Sir Purrcival springs to attention—eyes black, tail switching, claws flexing. Let that same dog intrude into Purrcival's territory, and he is not just on the defensive—he is downright aggressive.

Whoever heard of a cat keeping physically fit? Certainly not Purrcival, but he need make no apologies. Sprinting out through the door he confronts the dog head-on. Bewildered by this scratching, snarling bundle of fury, the dog yelps in dismay and flees for home.

Smug with victory, Sir Purrcival strolls leisurely back to his pillow, smooths his ruffled fur, and settles down to finish the catnap that was so rudely interrupted.

He is seldom bothered by the same dog twice.

One who rebukes boldly makes peace. —Proverbs 10:10

PURRables

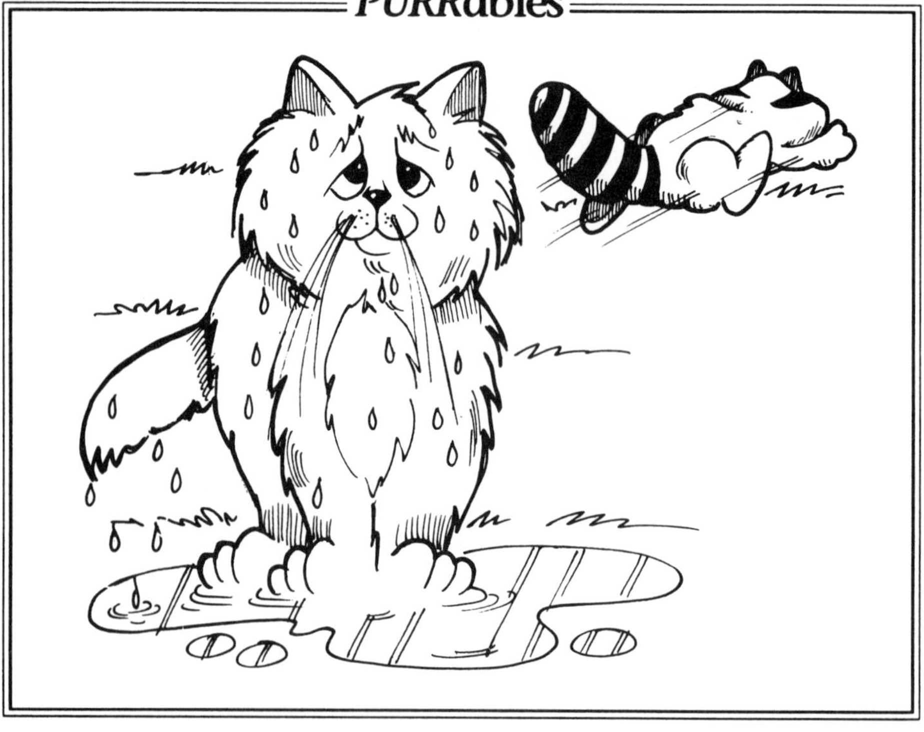

Tested–

My assumptions are based only on circumstantial evidence, but I believe Sir Purrcival has tangled with a raccoon. As if to substantiate my theory, the local paper this very day has cautioned pet owners to beware of these masked bandits. Just last evening a springer spaniel out walking along the river bank was taken hostage by a raccoon. Despite the owner's desperate attempts to break up the fight, the raccoon maneuvered the dog down to the water and drowned it before her very eyes.

Sir Purrcival, therefore, is probably luckier than he knows. He came home this morning soaked to the skin, his dignity suffering immeasurably from the ordeal. Not only that, but as I dry him off, I notice a distinct bite mark at the root of the old caudal appendage, severely limiting its flexibility.

You have no idea how irritable Sir Purrcival can be when his tail movements are restricted. He goes about with his flag at half mast, bemoaning his fate and soliciting salve and sympathy. Up to this point in time I was under the assumption that he was a big strong cat. Put to the test by that raccoon, however, he has mysteriously changed into a frail shadow of his usual robust self.

If thou faint in the day of adversity, thy strength is small. –Proverbs 24:10 KJV

Errant

Around the house Sir Purrcival is loathe to rest so much as one delicate foot on anything even *slightly* damp, but let him succumb to the call of the wild and he exercises no such inhibitions. He comes home in spring with wads of dried mud stuck to the bottom of his paws. Annoyed because such a foreign substance hampers his feline ability to pad noiselessly about the house, he proceeds to remove it.

Now none of us would consider mudballs for breakfast as very appetizing, nor does the tomcat. After removing the mud from between his toes, he spits it out in ever widening circles around the house, but *never* at the back entrance. He would rather sit outside and *starve* than pick his toes on the back door mat. To his way of thinking, that kind of behavior is typical of a dumb old dog who can be told what to do, and how, and when and where. As a cat, Sir Purrcival sees no reason whatever why he can't go where he pleases and do exactly as he likes, even if the consequences of his chosen course seriously jeopardize his relationship with the family.

Ponder the path of thy feet. —Proverbs 4:26 KJV

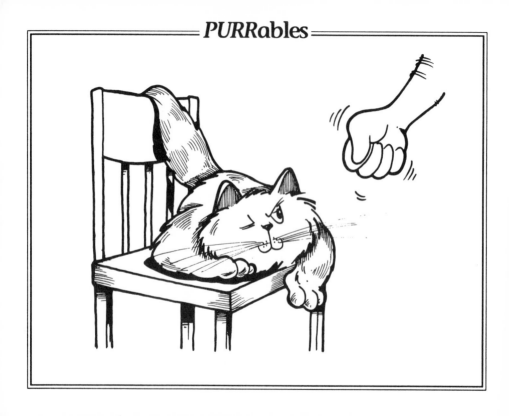

PURRables

Denounced–

I am catching forty winks in the afternoon when a loud rap on the door jolts me from my bed. A huge fellow with grizzled face fairly shouts at me, "Have you got a black cat?"

"No, I haven't," I reply, pointing to Sir Purrcival, calmly sleeping on a kitchen chair.

"Nah, that ain't the one." For Sir Purrcival's sake, I am very glad it isn't.

"Why are you looking for a black cat?"

"Because I live behind you and there's an (unprintable) black cat digging up my garden every night, that's why!"

There is such venom in his voice and vengeance in his eye I am *doubly* glad I don't own a black cat. I am glad I am not a cat, period.

He rants and raves about his precious garden being on the verge of death, in his estimation such a heinous crime that even capital punishment is too lenient for neighbors whose cats and dandelions roam at will. Guilty on both counts, I hastily shut the door in hopes of obtaining a stay of execution.

One given to anger stirs up strife, and the hothead causes much transgression.
—Proverbs 29:22

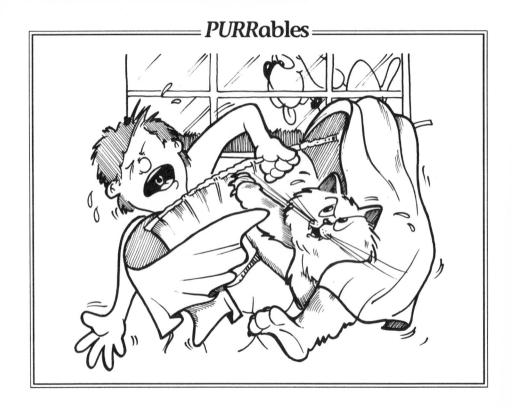

Revengeful—

In the wee hours of the morning Sir Purrcival happens to be sitting on the basement windowsill in our son's bedroom when who should come snooping around outside but the neighbor's dog, Smiley.

When Smiley sticks his nose against the windowpane, such impudence riles Sir Purrcival beyond measure. He lets out a blood curdling yowl that jolts our son straight from his sleep and sends him scrambling to the window. As he makes a grab for the cat, Sir Purrcival turns on him with claws outstretched and fangs bared. In the ensuing turmoil the curtain rod collapses and boy and cat and draperies are all tangled in one seething mass of fury.

Going down to restore order, I find our son vowing solemn revenge on Smiley the dog, who has been watching the whole fracas with amused expression. As for Purrcival, he can't *wait* to get his claws on that miserable pooch.

Naively unaware of what lies in store for him, Smiley trots off home wearing a silly canine grin and relishing fond memories of the scene he has just witnessed.

Those who are glad at calamity will not go unpunished. —Proverbs 17:5

*PURR*ables

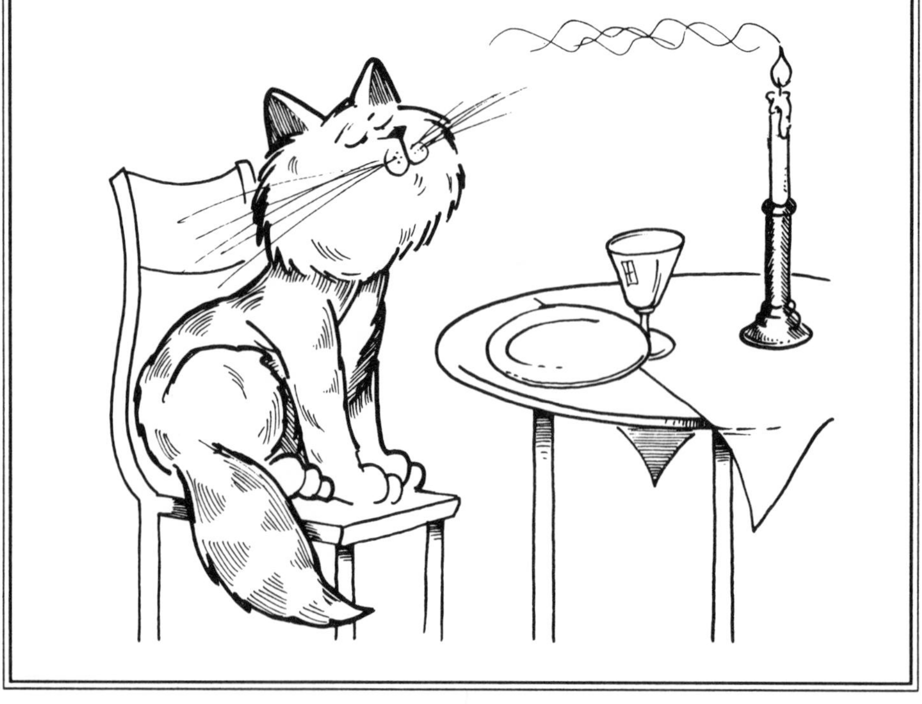

Slighted—

Sir Purrcival's demands for room service today are being ignored, and for very good reason.

His box of cat food is empty. Not prepared to take the chef's word for it, of course, he comes to the kitchen and peers into the empty box with one eye. Looks can deceive, so he reaches in with one paw. What a pity! It is indeed empty.

I suggest something from the regular menu, but he sniffs at my offer with disdain. An aristocratic tomcat does have his pride, you know. He will just sit here in the parlor and wait. Perchance one of these plebian servants coming to the back door will be so kind as to fetch him a box of cat food? Alas, neither the paper boy, the meter reader nor the mailman can be bribed.

Smarting from certain snide remarks about a proud feline who would rather die of malnutrition than condescend, Sir Purrcival finally deigns to throw himself upon the mercy of our teenage son. He reluctantly cycles "all the way to the store to get a stupid box of food for a despicable dumb old cat!"

Better to be despised and have a servant than to be self important and lack food. —Proverbs 12:9

Chastened—

Despite dismal failures in the past to exercise the proper decorum at meal time, Sir Purrcival is wondering how to wheedle out another invitation to dinner.

If he wants to observe this ritual firsthand, maybe he should wash his face before meal time without being told, which is more than can be said for the kids in the family.

And then *purr*haps if he quietly sits down on the vacant chair, and behaves superbly, he *might* be allowed to grace the dinner table with his presence during the entire meal.

Even the family critics have to concede that Sir Purrcival is exhibiting remarkable self discipline during the first course. Only the very perceptive person would notice the momentary dilation of his pupils, the sudden impulse to pounce upon that which pleases the palate.

When the plate of meat passes before his very eyes, however, Sir Purrcival just can't resist putting two front paws on the edge of the table. Such behavior is immediately deemed a definite breach of etiquette. Once again Sir Purrcival is sent from the table until he learns better manners.

Reproofs of discipline are the way of life. —Proverbs 6:23

PURRables

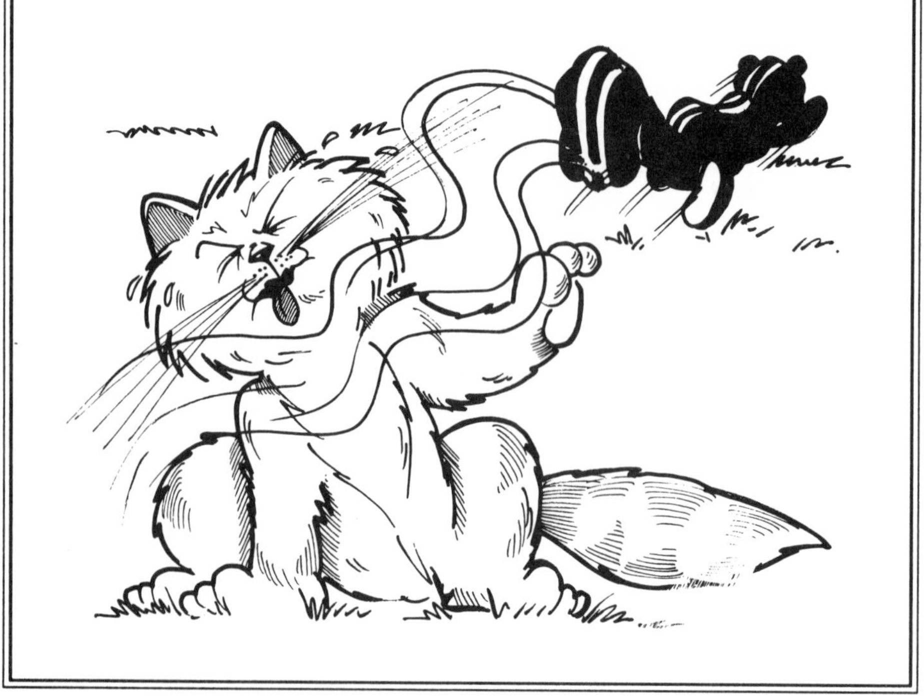

Tainted—

Come the morning, we open the door and in bounds Sir Purrcival, reeking from a recent rendezvous with a *skunk*. Sometime during the wee hours of the night he must have pressed his luck one paw too far with that cute little black and white kitty, and now he is saturated with "Her Highness Cologne."

Holding our noses, we banish him from the house, his dish being the only item that is sent into exile with him.

Later, much later, when the family has gone their separate ways, I very discreetly open the door. Sir Purrcival slips into the basement. The odor of skunk has dissipated considerably, but not enough to make him socially acceptable.

Have you ever given a cat a sponge bath? With tomato juice? Neither had I, until today. At first Purrcival is exceptionally cooperative, for a cat. I swab and he licks, but it is a tedious chore. Long before I am finished, however, Sir Purrcival considers himself *purr*fectly presentable. No amount of arguing can convince him otherwise, even though lingering traces of skunk still follow him wherever he goes.

There are those who are pure in their own eyes yet are not cleansed of their filthiness. —Proverbs 30:12

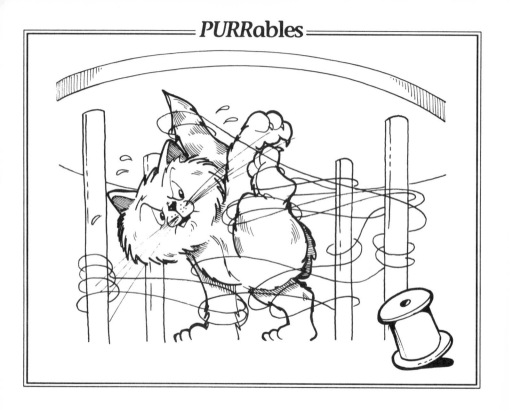

Entangled—

The whole family has succumbed to the flu. Creaking and moaning and rasping for relief, we sound like victims of the bubonic plague.

The tomcat remains in fine fettle, making his rounds to the sickbeds at regular intervals. Failing to solicit much response, he decides to embark into the sewing room on a little foray all his own.

What captures his attention is the thread on the sewing machine, and he begins unwinding it at a very rapid rate. From somewhere in the depths of my flu-induced stupor, I hear the sound of the spool spinning. By the time I rally to my senses, Purrcival has disappeared.

Light-headed and bleary-eyed, I try to focus on the trail of thread, vaguely hoping that sooner or later I will find a cat at the end of it. I finally track him down in the dining room, where he has effectively tethered himself to the table leg by getting tangled up in yards and yards of thread. Not in the least worried about the possible consequences, he has a ball of fun poking at my scissors as I cut him free.

It is like sport to a fool to do mischief. —Proverbs 10:23 KJV

PURRables

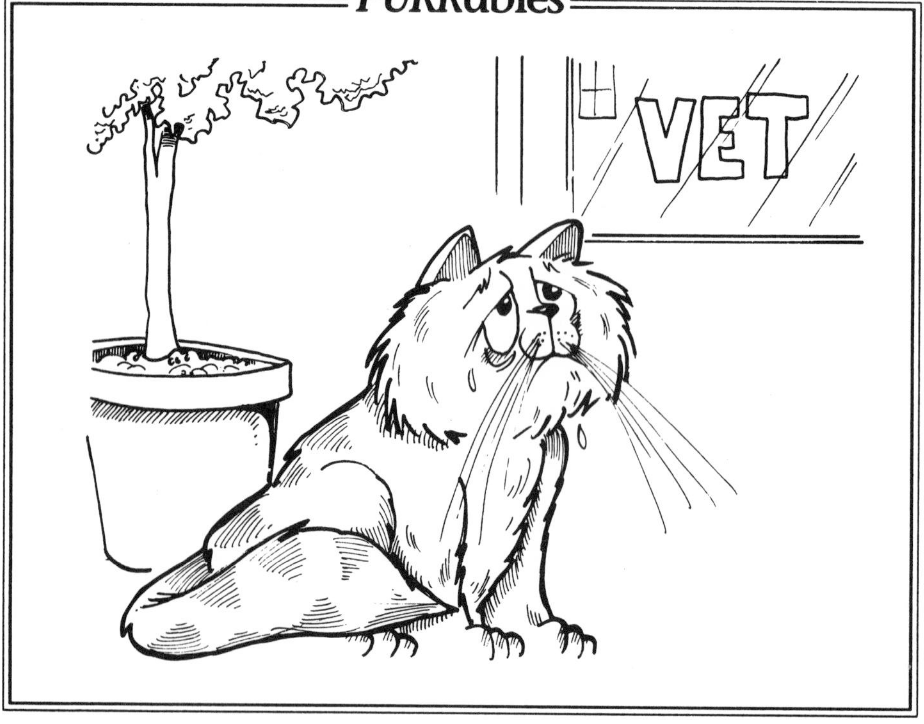

Ailing—

Swallowing a foreign object does strange things to a cat's constitution, none of which are very pleasant.

The vet tells me to bring him in for observation. He thinks Purrcival may have swallowed a needle, but X-rays show nothing metallic lodged in his intestines.

If he has swallowed thread, the vet is even more concerned. To use his terminology, "a cat's gut works like a concertina, and a piece of thread can cut through the bellows." Up until now, I had been given to understand that cat innards were used exclusively for *fiddle* music. Now I am being told that I actually own a one-cat Cajun band, except that Purrcival is just not *purr*forming up to par.

Preparing to do exploratory surgery, the vet administers an anesthetic, but just prior to making the incision, he probes around once more in Purrcival's throat. And there he finds it—the lost cord, a piece of thread wound tightly around the cat's tongue and interfering with the natural rhythm of his digestive system.

Purrcival's constitution quickly returns to peak performance. As for that conscientious vet, the tomcat owes him his undying appreciation. I owe him considerably more.

Those who are attentive to a matter will prosper. –Proverbs 16:20

Dispatched—

When it comes to the serious matter of diet, Sir Purrcival is not only precise. He is punctual. First thing every morning he plucks at the screen door with his center claw, we let him in, and he trots directly to his dish.

Come evening, he likes nothing better than to watch friend hubby mix up a jug of powdered milk, captivated by the froth that forms at the top. Perhaps Sir Purrcival's ancestors were common barn cats who lurked around the pail at milking time. For someone of Sir Purrcival's prestige the very idea is preposterous, but at the same time he cannot resist the smell of warm milk. He joyously partakes for the last time on Friday evening, washes his whiskers and walks out into the night.

The next morning we find his lifeless body lying along the roadside, all evidence indicating that he has been killed instantaneously by a speeding driver.

He is laid to rest out where the wild roses bloom, the raindrops blending with our tears. It is a private interment ceremony, since few and far between are those who are prepared to eulogize a dead tomcat. Indeed, the majority of people consider our loss so irrelevant as to be unworthy of any sympathy whatsoever. And so we stoically shroud our sorrow behind our smiles and carry on with life.

Even in laughter the heart may be in pain. —Proverbs 14:13 NAS

Losing a friend...

Remembering—

The shock of losing Sir Purrcival Van Mouser has not yet worn off when a neighbor brings me a cactus in full bloom. She doesn't really *say* that it's an expression of sympathy, but some things don't have to be said in order to be understood.

After she is gone, I water it with tears.

No plant from the entire field of horticulture could better memorialize Sir Purrcival than a cactus. Sitting on the windowsill soaking up the sunshine, it is a constant reminder of his thorny disposition, his dry feline wit, his rugged constitution.

Other cats were sociable. Sir Purrcival was a rugged individualist. To his way of thinking, utter surrender to domesticity was unthinkable; forfeiting the call of the wild unbearable. He would tolerate surprising extremes in the elements, but like the cactus, he flourished best in the hot sun, soaking up its rays from every angle. And although he bloomed but briefly, he left behind some vivid memories, and then was buried in the shifting sands of time.

The landscape seems a barren place without him.

By sorrow of heart the spirit is broken. —Proverbs15:13

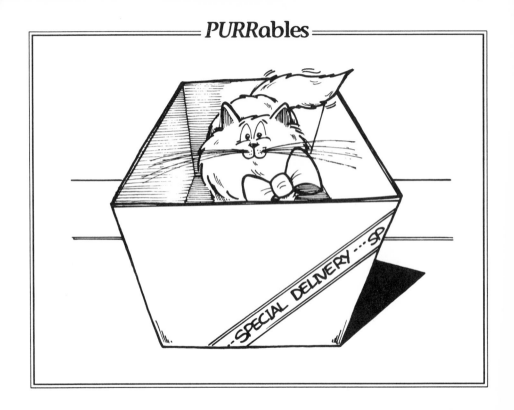

Replaced—

When a speeding motorist shamelessly refused to grant the right of way to our dearly beloved Sir Purrcival, it was a venerable member of the Van Mouser dynasty who found himself hastened to feline heaven.

His detractors may have mentally assigned him a place in *purr*gatory, but be that as it may, underneath that furry countenance and fuzzy paws there lurked as respectable a set of fangs and claws as ever roamed a neighborhood. Every time he asked to go out I felt guilty placing the birds in such jeopardy, because he could be a very self-sufficient cat.

In more congenial moods, however, he was an excellent companion, and as they say of the noble, "a constant source of in*spurr*ation."

I begin to look for a successor, but the task is more difficult than I imagine. All sorts of cats and kittens are being thrust forward as pretenders to the throne, but none show much potential. A friend assures us that she has finally made connections with just the right cat. A few days later little Sir Purrcival van Mouser II is hand delivered right to our door, complete with a bow around his neck and a complimentary can of cat food.

We extend a hearty welcome.

A gift opens doors; it gives access to the great. —Proverbs 18:16

Undisciplined—

Little Sir Purrcival II is nothing much more than two blueberry eyes propelled by a ball of fluff, but we can see that he has the makings of a great tomcat. He toddles off down the hall on a spindly set of bowed legs and comes back looking for a bite to eat. Even a crumb of bread is guarded with fierce tenacity for one so young. When teased, he reacts with miniature snarls and hisses.

Come bedtime, he is as compliant as a hyperactive cactus, his thorny claws and sharp teeth penetrating the covers at unpredictable times and places. Banished to his basket for bad behavior, he meows plaintively until someone takes pity on his plight.

I fear little Sir Purrcival is a kitten only a family of cat lovers could raise. His unprovoked hissing terrifies visitors. His uncoordinated claws make shreds of their sweaters. He is apt to sink his fangs into unsuspecting ankles. Such juvenile behavior is certainly earning little Sir Purrcival a reputation, but it is not exactly praiseworthy.

Even a child is known by his doings. —Proverbs 20:11 KJV

PURRables

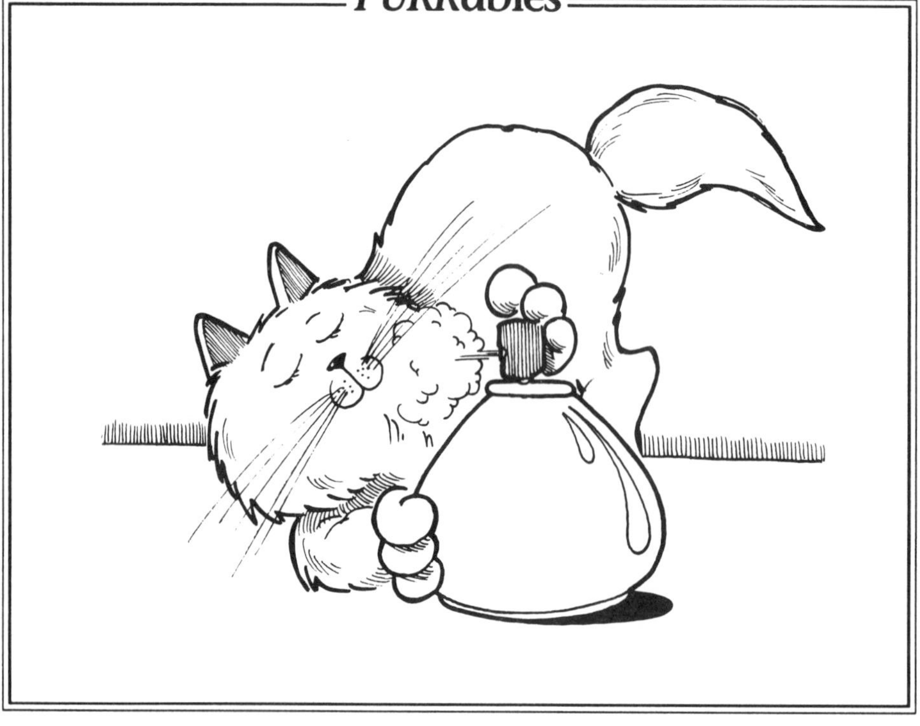

Charming—

It's one of those mornings when I wake up and wish mirrors had never been invented. My hair looks like it was combed with an egg beater, I have blotches on my face from an uneven tan, and my fingernails are ravaged from grating carrots. My slacks have baggy knees, my sweater is stained with orange juice, and there's a hole in my slipper.

In the midst of wondering how to salvage the shreds of my self-esteem, I happen to notice little Sir Purrcival furtively sneaking under the bed. Just when I get down among the dust balls to try and ascertain whether he has ulterior motives for hiding there, the doorbell rings.

Ding-dong. Guess who's calling? I just *know* it has to be one of those spiffy women peddling cosmetics, the kind who float up to my door in a cloud of perfume.

I wiggle out backwards from under the bed, disengage the kitten from my sweater, brush the dustballs from my knees and limp to the front door minus one slipper. I fully expect the cosmetics lady to run the other way, except that she is absolutely enamored by cute little Sir Purrcival. And allured by all the exotic fragrances she carries, Purrcival reciprocates in kind. As a result, the three of us spend a pleasant and profitable hour together.

Perfume and incense make the heart glad. —Proverbs 27:9

Quarrelsome–

We go to sleep with the sound of a gentle rain pitter-pattering on the roof. By morning there is the cushioned silence that spells the ominous presence of snow. Nature has done an early test run on winter.

In contrast to that peaceful landscape outside, the household is in a state of frenzy. Everyone starts a frantic search for boots, mittens and scarves. Flashlights are at a premium as the kids rummage around in dark closets, squabbling over the ownership of anything which even remotely resembles last winter's apparel. Eventually the trail of cast off, rejected, outgrown, or otherwise unsuitable attire stretches from an upstairs closet all the way down the stairs, around the corner, and into the basement boot cupboard.

Purrcival the kitten is on a real rampage. He's never seen so many mittens to chew, laces to tangle or scarves to swing from. And best of all, everybody is in a super mood to FIGHT! By the time the kids leave for school, Purrcival has managed to undermine every ounce of admiration he has hitherto enjoyed, just because he is so quick at pouncing on every opportunity to aggravate an already tense situation.

One who dwells on disputes will alienate a friend. –Proverbs17:9b

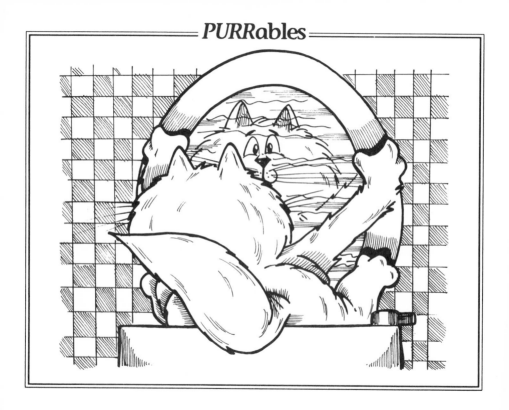

Reflective—

It is not unusual to walk into the bathroom only to find young Purrcival perched up on the rim of the toilet, gazing steadfastly into the depths below. He is spellbound watching his own reflection in the water. For all he knows, he is the only cat alive, a prospect both intriguing and scary.

When he meets another feline firsthand, he is both shocked and puzzled. It *looks* like his reflection, but it isn't. The other cat is assuming a similar posture, only on a larger scale. It arches its back like he does. The hair rises along its spine. Its eyes bug out like his do. Its whiskers twitch. Its tail stiffens up like a bottle brush.

After a few seconds of looking mutually foolish, the fears of both cats slowly dissipate. Their backs relax, their stares soften, and tails gradually resume normal proportions. They seem to agree that they have quite a bit in common after all. Instead of watching his reflection in water, little Sir Purrcival has actually seen himself in another cat, and what an eye opener that has been!

Just as water reflects the face, so one. . . heart reflects another. —Proverbs 27:19

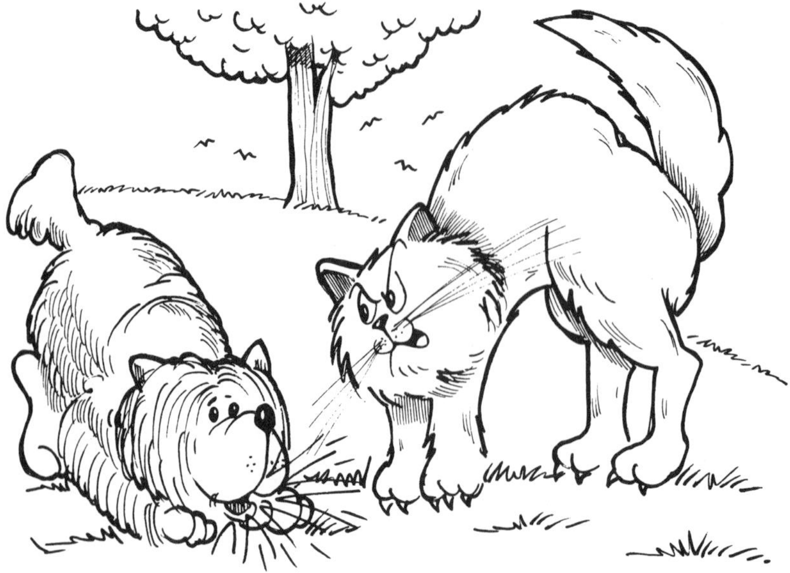

Riled—

Young Purrcival just happens to be in a feisty mood the day Woofus the dog puts in an appearance.

Young Purrcival has never before been exposed to anything even faintly resembling a canine, and Woofus only faintly resembles one. He looks more like a mobile mop, and when he comes dusting up the driveway Purrcival thinks the heat is causing hallucinations. Here is this hairy-looking creature making the wildest noises he has ever heard. Every time Woofus barks, Purrcival jumps straight in the air. *Bark!* Jump! *Bark!* Jump!

Purrcival's feline temper is rising higher all the time. Knowing Woofus the dog, I realize that the cat is in no real physical danger. Should I at least try to salvage his dignity?

I fear I am already too late. Purrcival's eyes are bugged out, his fangs bared, his back arched, his tail enormous, and he is standing on the very tip of his toenails, absolutely *glaring* at Woofus the dog, who is calmly grinning back at him. Since Purrcival is suffering nothing more than painful humiliation brought on by quick temper, I decide to let him extricate himself from his dilemma as best he can.

. . . great anger shall bear the penalty. If you rescue him, you will only have to do it again. —Proverbs 19:19 NAS

Insensitive—

At Christmas time our son sweeps the tomcat up in his arms and insists that Purrcival help him sing a duet. Exhibiting the typical false modesty that one has come to expect from performers, the cat waits to be coaxed. Impatient to get on with the show, however, our son simply pinches Purrcival's tail at the appropriate point in the music. Together they sing an acceptable rendition of "Go tell it on the (pinch) *MEOW*ntain, over the hills and everywhere . . . ."

A reluctant caroller at Christmas time, Sir Purrcival does an about face come spring. When he gets on the back fence at three in the morning, serenading his latest heart throb, he seems to think he's a topnotch tenor, a veritable "*Purr*varotti" of cats. As such, he cannot understand why anyone, even neighbors wakened from the deepest of sleep, should be so irate. They hurl stinging insults in his direction, forcing his performance to an untimely finish. Even his very own family, so wearied by the cares of this life, are not in the least uplifted by his superb talent and exquisite lyrics. Quite the contrary.

Like vinegar on a wound is one who sings songs to a heavy heart. —Proverbs 25:20

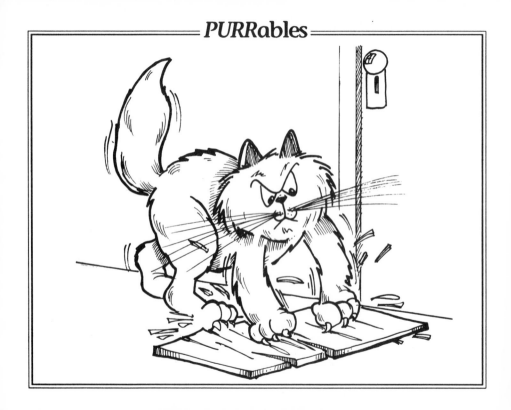

Inconsolable—

My handsome young tomcat has come to the attention of ardent females, and he comes home day after day bearing battle scars inflicted by jealous suitors. Concerned that he might succumb to a fatal infection with all those punctures and claw marks, I swab his torn wounds with disinfectant, "*purr*oxide" of course.

I phone the vet, who agrees that a little operation is in order. The instructions are explicit: No cat yummies after 6 p.m., no milk after midnight, keep Sir Purrcival inside until morning and have him to the clinic by eight. Now the tomcat can ignore his calcium quota, he can even bypass his cat yummies, but don't try to keep him inside on a spring night. No self-respecting suitor is going to sleep in the rocking chair while his current heart throb sits on the back fence and wails in lonely anguish over her plight.

Back and forth Sir Purrcival roams, his indignant yowls piercing the wee hours of the morning and shattering sleep. I hear him investigate every possibility of escape, testing the security of doors and windows with outstretched claws. When none gives way, he vents his fury on the door mat, leaving it a hopeless tangle of snags. At 4 a.m. I finally lure him into fitful sleep on his favorite blanket, an exhausted, brokenhearted feline wallowing in the depths of despair.

Hope deferred makes the heart sick. —Proverbs 13:12

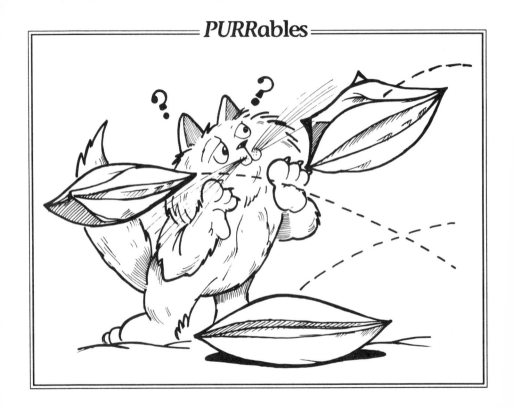

Misunderstood—

Like most early risers, Sir Purrcival is not content to keep quiet about it. Just to make *doubly* certain that the members of his immediate household do not overlook such rare virtue, he assumes the position of mobile alarm clock.

Were we not somewhat prejudiced to the service he so willingly provides, we would see that he is uniquely equipped for the job—self-winding movement, glow in the dark face, padded feet, and *very* punctual timing. Not only that, but as he paces up and down the hall at the snap of sunrise, his loud, intermittent meowing works every bit as well, if not *better,* than any snooze and wake button.

One by one he escorts the sleepyheads to the breakfast table. However, he can never understand why they are so out-of-sorts with him. Has he not done an outstanding job of waking them up at the very beginning of a brand new day? Will they not thank him for getting them off to such an early start? But no! There they sit, loudly berating him for doing them a good turn. Sir Purrcival is miffed. *One would expect these human beings to show some appreciation.*

On second thought, *purr*haps 5 a.m. is a tad early, but how was he to know they wanted to sleep in on Saturday?

He who blesses his friend with a loud voice early in the morning, it will be reckoned a curse to him. —Proverbs 27:14 NAS

Conscientious–

Being a nocturnal sort, Sir Purrcival feels compelled to roam all night, even in the depths of winter; but then he comes home in the morning and sleeps for the better part of the day.

Later on in the afternoons, when the weather warms up and conditions are a little more tolerable, Sir Purrcival may ease himself up onto the window ledge to take stock of the bird-feeder. If there are any of those black-capped chickadees around it's a sure sign the concrete steps won't be getting any warmer, and less conscientious cats will stay in where it's warm.

But somebody has to patrol the neighborhood to keep the varmints under control. So come night time, Sir Purrcival will once more step out into the dark cold night, for duty calls. Long lonely hours on the graveyard shift eventually gnaw away at anybody's morale, however, and Sir Purrcival is no exception. By morning, his sad complaints will again be the cue that he is in dire need of immediate restorative measures. In lieu of more specialized treatment, food and rest are *purr*fectly acceptable.

The Lord will not suffer the soul of the righteous to famish . . . . –Proverbs 10:3 KJV

Obstinate—

In the interest of conserving heat loss, the experts are always reminding us to buy energy-efficient homes. That may be fine, but I wish they would also tell me how to program the tomcat so he wouldn't go in and out so often in the middle of winter.

If he would zip through the doorway with the same agility he reserves for robins, I would have fewer complaints. But no! Come cold weather, he thinks he has to acclimatize gradually, daily easing himself out into the wintry scene with due and proper caution. In the meantime, he vehemently denies my allegations that he is responsible for all the warm air rapidly escaping through the open door.

The heat loss would be reduced by half if Sir Purrcival had no tail. Inching the old caudal appendage out the door consumes as much time as getting his body through. Those who suggest I speed him on his way with the aid of my foot have never tangled with my tomcat. In surly mood he is apt to turn and plunge his fangs right through my slippers.

A scoffer who is rebuked will only hate you. —Proverbs 9:8

Grasping—

Somewhere in his noble ancestry there must have been a feline who guarded the riches of nobility with fierce tenacity. Sir Purrcival has inherited his genes. Let him be within reach of anything I claim as "Mine!" and a low rumble in his throat erupts into a full scale growl and then escalates to a hiss. Vicious claws encircle the coveted treasure and four sharp fangs secure it for safety.

Never mind that the treasure is as worthless to me as to Sir Purrcival—a crumpled piece of paper, a plastic bag, a pencil stub. The tomcat has to prove a point. If somebody challenges the ownership by saying, "Mine!" he immediately lays claim.

Whether it rightfully belongs to him or not, or whether he even has any use for it, is a moot point. His grasping *attitude* is what causes dissension. I am frequently called upon to arbitrate disputes, simply because various members of the family cannot refrain from challenging a big fat cat, if for no other reason than to expose the worst side of his character.

Those who are greedy for unjust gain make trouble for their households.
—Proverbs15:27a

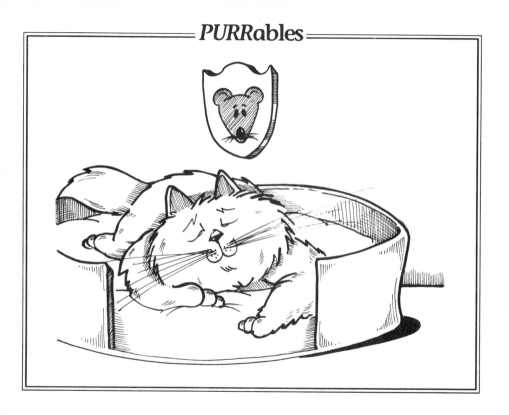

Long Suffering—

For some reason, friend hubby and Sir Purrcival both lay claim to the same easy chair at the same moment in time, which always creates somewhat of a scene. Being bigger and louder, friend hubby usually wins. But being stubborn and proud, Sir Purrcival never surrenders. This inevitably leads to all sorts of sarcastic rejoinders.

"That foul feline!" declares friend hubby. "He wouldn't know a mouse if he saw one."

Sir Purrcival gazes off into the distance, a glint of resentment in his great green eyes. Sometimes there's a limit to what a cat can take.

Today our son comes charging into the house. "Mom! Mom! There's a dead mouse on the grass. We oughta have it bronzed! Dad's *never* gonna believe this!"

He doesn't, either. He claims the mouse died of old age while tottering across the lawn.

As for Sir Purrcival, he maintains a cool detachment, satisfied that the trophy-sized specimen he has just dragged home is more than enough evidence to silence his major detractors, of whom there is at least one.

The prudent ignore an insult. —Proverbs 12:16

Obstructive–

Friend hubby decides to assemble my new bird-feeder, so I follow him down to his work bench. Sir Purrcival promptly stations himself in the middle of the proceedings to make sure we do it right.

We don't. We can't find the correct screws, and the nail heads are too small. The tomcat is in the way and we can't see properly so we need the trouble light, which we can't find.

Three hours later I'm beginning to wonder whether it was such a good idea after all, but the tomcat seems to think it is the best bird-baiter he has ever helped nail together.

We carry the new feeder to a strategic spot in the backyard for the grand unveiling, fill it with bird seed and wait for some feathered friends to land.

Day one–No birds. Day two–Ditto. And little wonder. Sir Purrcival thinks it is his *purr*ogative to station himself full length across the adjacent picnic table (appropriately named) in hopes that a hungry bird will fall into his mitt. Seeing those lethal jaws just waiting to spring, the birds are staying away in droves.

In vain is the net baited while the bird is looking on. –Proverbs 1:17

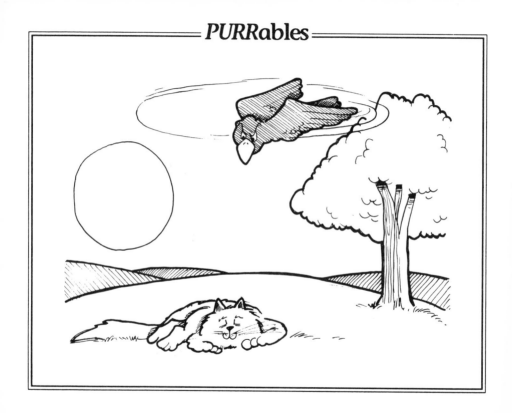

Unintimidated—

Casper the crow was barely hatched last year when a neighborhood boy tamed him and taught him to say a few raucous words in exchange for a crust of bread. At that time Sir Purrcival was just a little kitten, but since kittens and crusts appeared equally appetizing to that crow, I had to be certain I had a piece of bread in my pocket whenever Casper landed in for lunch. Strutting over to my outstretched hand, he would snatch the crust and gobble it down with gusto.

One thing is certain. A crow at close range does not resemble a canary. Long curved beak, flashing mean eyes, bristly black plumage—Casper looked like blackmail incorporated, a cantankerous villain whom I secretly detested but whom I dared not ignore for little Sir Purrcival's sake.

A year later, however, I am no longer forced to bargain with crusts whenever I hear a caw. That vulnerable little kitten I once had to protect has now grown into a muscular twelve-pound tomcat who considers himself the undisputed monarch of the jungle. As he proudly guards the site of an imaginary kill, he is not intimidated in the least by the ominous sight of a circling black vulture. Should that puny crow ever dare to land, he would be lucky indeed to escape with tailfeathers intact.

The lion . . . does not turn back before any. —Proverbs 30:30

Independent—

While we are away on vacation, the tomcat is living alone, and I wonder how he is faring. Is he suffering from dehydration in the hot sun on the back step? Gaunt from lack of food? Soaked in a summer rain? Like a king who has been banished into exile, Sir Purrcival is not accustomed to the denial of privileges. When we return I expect to find, at best, an emaciated mouser pleading for reinstatement. At worst I am afraid we might find his dead body lying where it has fallen in battle.

As we swing into the driveway after a week's absence, the car lights reveal no such tragic consequences. Instead, Sir Purrcival slowly emerges from his summer quarters on the back porch, a luxurious stretch indicating he has just bedded down for the night on his cozy woollen blanket. For an entire week he has been basking in the attentions lavished on him by an admiring neighbor. Accustomed as he is to such homage, he regards our homecoming as nothing more than the rude intrusion of menial subjects clamoring for admittance to his palace. Our straggly appearance dictates that we be escorted to the back door. As Sir Purrcival struts impatiently along at the head of the procession, a haughty jerk in the crook of his tail conveys his deep displeasure that the days of his solitary reign are all but over.

The one who lives alone is self-indulgent. —Proverbs 18:1

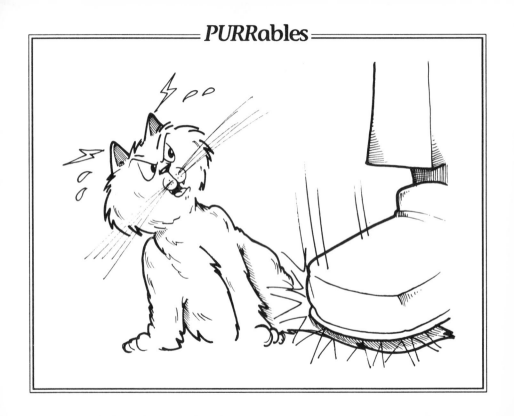

Irritated—

Long and elegant as it is, Sir Purrcival's tail grabs the attention of every sticky-fisted little toddler who ever visits, and cleaning dried teething biscuits from his fur is a task he would rather avoid.

He is also suspect of any pesky little girl who tries to lull him to sleep in her lap. When he wakes up he is apt to find himself in her doll carriage with a bonnet over his ears and a bow tied on his tail. The ignominy is unbearable.

At the other end of the spectrum, some sadistic little villain may suddenly damage his ego in a different sort of way by delivering a karate chop to his tail when nobody is looking.

Purely in deference to all such visitors who don't know any better, Sir Purrcival maintains a surprising amount of decorum. But should a member of the immediate household accidentally trample the old tail underfoot, Sir Purrcival vents his full and furious indignation. *As if she can't see a great big fat cat sitting right here in the way! The very idea!* Convinced that there is no excuse whatever for such disgraceful behavior, Sir Purrcival's reaction is both prompt and painful.

Wrath falls on one who acts shamefully. —Proverbs 14:35

Exasperating–

This morning, Sir Purrcival's intention to curl up on the bed for a good long rest happened to conflict with our plans to lay a new carpet in the bedroom.

We soon discover that coaxing a cat to exercise mind-over-mattress is a lesson in futility. Purrcival is bound to sleep in the middle of that bed, and it matters little that we think otherwise. As fast as we lift him down, he gets back up again. We cannot lock him out of the bedroom—we have already removed the door. We cannot lock him out of the house—the entrance is jammed with bedroom furniture. So, if a double mattress and box spring aren't heavy enough to lift as one unit, there is a twelve-pound tomcat added to the load.

By the time we get the carpet laid, re-arrange the bedroom furniture, and put the door back on its hinges, we are about to collapse from exhaustion. But there is still one supreme effort to be made, that of shifting both bed and tomcat back into position. Just as we are finished, the obese old ingrate wakes up, gives a perfunctory sniff of all our hard work and promptly asks to be excused.

I gladly show him the door.

A stone is heavy, and sand is weighty, but a fool's provocation is heavier than both. —Proverbs 27:3

*PURR*ables

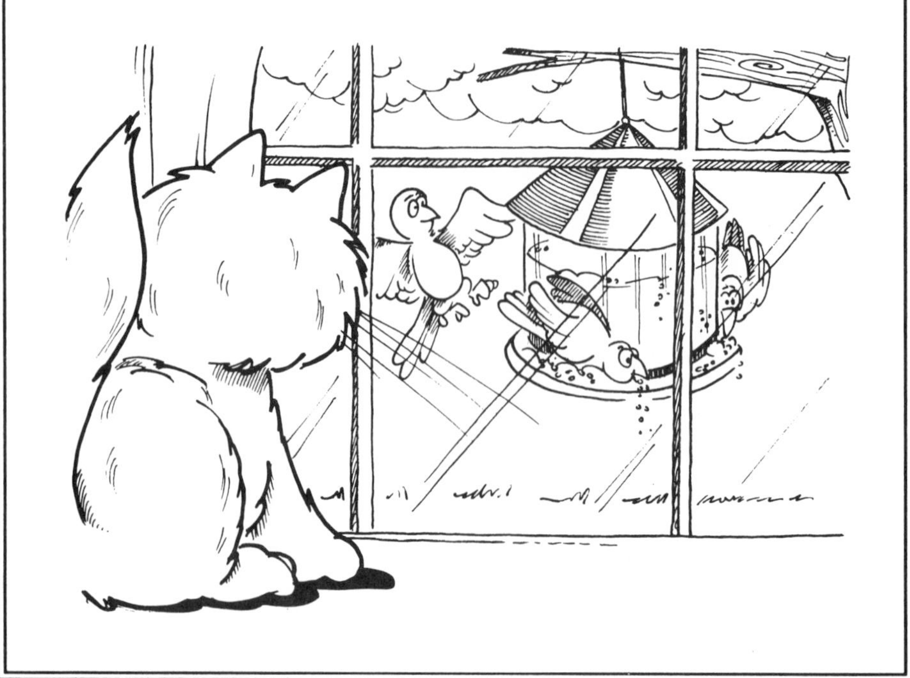

Scheming—

If it is a very cold morning, Sir Purrcival curls up in his basket to await the day's developments.

Perhaps it will snow and some of those big white flakes will come drifting toward the window. Difficult to catch, but fun to watch. A little like feathers.

Ah, yes! Feathers. Despite years of domestication, Sir Purrcival's primeval hunting instincts are still aroused by the sight of a single bird at the feeder. He flattens his ears and clacks his teeth and generally threatens to exterminate every creature that has ever hatched within a five mile radius.

But it has been a long hard winter, and Sir Purrcival has never found it so difficult to spot a good plump specimen of birdhood. Therefore, when a family of sparrows lands at the feeder, innocently fluttering and chirping within a few feet of the cat's nose, Sir Purrcival is doubly determined to round out his menu with a choice pair of sparrow drumsticks. So intense is his concentration that he dare not even lick his whiskers in anticipation, but keeps his mouth tightly closed, the better to conceal his deadly schemes.

One who compresses the lips brings evil to pass. —Proverbs 16:30b

Humiliated—

Hoping to play a practical trick on the tomcat, somebody buys a battery-operated bird to hang on the Christmas tree. Sir Purrcival is no fool. He is not about to forfeit his proud feline dignity at the best of times, and *certainly* not in the presence of Christmas company.

On the other hand, a partridge in a pear tree *does* pose distinct possibilities. If he just waits until an opportune moment, *purr*chance he can catch his own festive meal.

And so Sir Purrcival bides his time until mere mortals are all fast asleep, poor things. Let the plebians dream of roast turkey while they can. A feline of Sir Purrcival's stature expects to partake of more exotic fare. Curled up in the big armchair, he is watching the tinsel quiver on the Christmas tree and debating his best move. I can picture what happens next. The quizzical black eyes, the slight switch of the tail, the crouch, and then the POUNCE!

The next thing I hear is a SWOOSH, tinkle, tinkle, followed by the screeching of the tomcat's claws slipping on the floor as he tries to make a fast but very undignified getaway from under the fallen Christmas tree.

Pride goes before destruction, and a haughty spirit before a fall. —Proverbs 16:18

PURRables

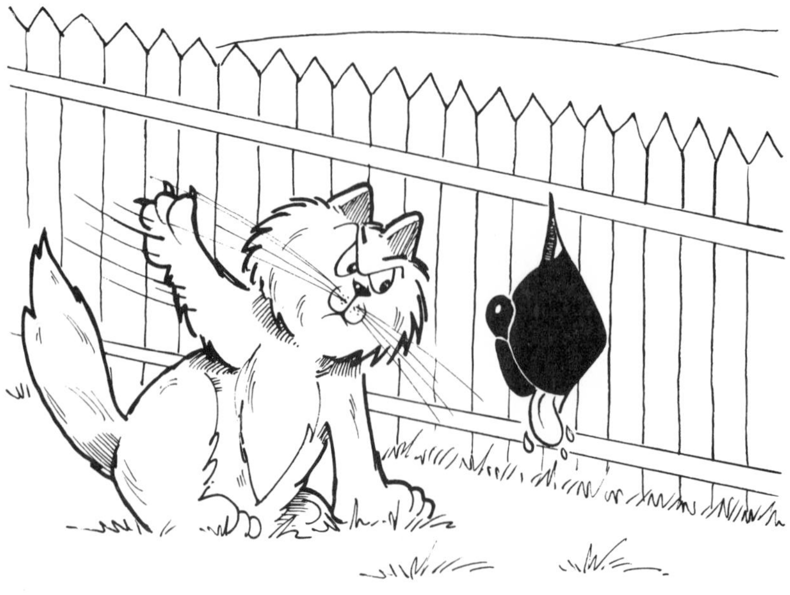

Prejudiced—

As if coping with the neighbor's dog to the north wasn't exasperating enough for Sir Purrcival. The folks to the south have brought home a mischievous black pup. Now Purrcival has to keep vigil over both sides of the property to make certain Gunnar (the retriever) and Thor (the terrior) don't trespass.

With both dogs sporting Scandinavian names, Purrcival fully expects they will come exploring at every opportunity. Like Eric-the-Red and Leif-the-Lucky, isn't it highly probable that a couple of canine Vikings called Gunnar and Thor will try to lay claim to Sir Purrcival's domain?

Gunnar has actually been skirting these shores for several years now, sailing back and forth along the north edge of the garden. He is kept at bay only by Sir Purrcival's hostile attitude, which strongly conveys the message that no canine visitors are welcome, friendly or otherwise.

But Thor, trusting young mutt that he is, sometimes ventures dangerously near the lot line. Should he ever land anywhere within reach, that rubber nose of his will be torn to shreds by Sir Purrcival, who presumes every dog is like every other dog— all of them snoopy canine encroachers.

Through presumption comes nothing but strife. —Proverbs 13:10 NAS

Clever—

Sir Purrcival has learned how to retrieve, but for ulterior purposes.

Friend hubby gets highly irate if he discovers a cat on the bed, an intolerance of which Sir Purrcival is well aware. Rather than being banished unceremoniously from the premises, Sir Purrcival has learned to wheedle his way into friend hubby's good graces by fetching a peace-offering at bed time. It may be nothing more than a crinkled bit of paper, or a twist tie, but Purrcival drops it on the bedspread and waits. Friend hubby then tosses it across the room and Purrcival brings it back time and again.

Should friend hubby drop off to sleep in the middle of this little retrieving game, Sir Purrcival himself suddenly gets very, very tired, too tired to even move off the bed. Now fast asleep, friend hubby is none the wiser.

If he *does* awaken, however, any feline who treasures all of his nine lives had better make himself scarce! Either that, or Sir Purrcival had better find another peace-offering quickly.

Last night he bounded up on the bed in the dark with a whole banana he had swiped from the kitchen table.

A gift in secret averts anger. —Proverbs 21:14

PURRables

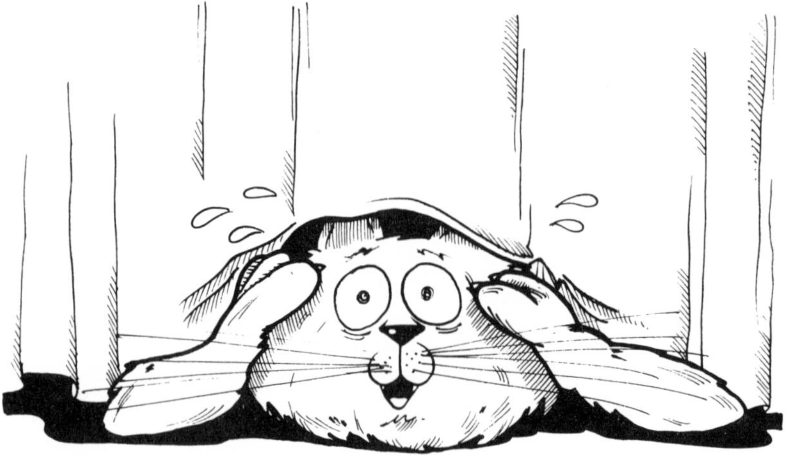

Cautious—

Sir Purrcival happens to be sitting on the arm of the easy chair, gazing out the front window, when a huge moving van comes rolling down the street. That in itself is such a rare occurrence in this neighborhood that Sir Purrcival has never seen the likes. *Why, a hapless feline caught under such big wheels would be flattened out like a gingerbread cat.* The very thought of it is enough to make Sir Purrcival uneasy. But when the moving van comes to an abrupt halt in front of our house, the loud hiss of the air brakes triggers off absolute alarm.

No doubt thinking he is about to be attacked by the biggest feline foe he has ever laid eyes upon, Purrcival skids down the hall in a state of panic. Desperately looking for a place to hide, he darts under the bed.

Since I have no way of telling him that he is just overreacting to the hiss of air brakes on a truck that is long since gone, he refuses to come out of hiding. Despite all my coaxing, he peers out at me skeptically from time to time, the bedspread draped over his vigilant ears. *A fellow can never tell when that big moving van may roll back in the opposite direction, flattening every cat within its path.*

The clever see danger and hide. —Proverbs 22:3

Distressed—

When I notice Purrcival making extended efforts to answer the call of nature, I attribute it to bashful kidney syndrome. But even when I surreptitiously peek at him from behind the venetian blind, I realize his little constitutional strolls are of no avail.

You know how it is. The drain never clogs until the plumber has packed up his pipe wrenches for the week, and the tomcat exhibits none of the above signs of distress until the vet has gone off duty. Concerned that Purrcival's waterworks might cease functioning altogether, we hustle him off to an emergency animal clinic.

The vet explains that a buildup of sediment is creating a blockage and that Purrcival will have to be treated under observation. Purrcival resists confinement in this strange place, especially with so many *dogs* in close proximity. *Any one of those great ravenous wolves could devour a sick cat with one gulp. And the racket they make!* The fact that a frightened Purrcival does not empty his bladder right on the spot is proof positive that the vet's diagnosis is correct.

Still, I hate to leave him there among strangers. As I walk to the car, there is a heavy lump of growing uncertainty pressing against my chest.

Anxiety weighs down the human heart. —Proverbs 12:25

PURRables

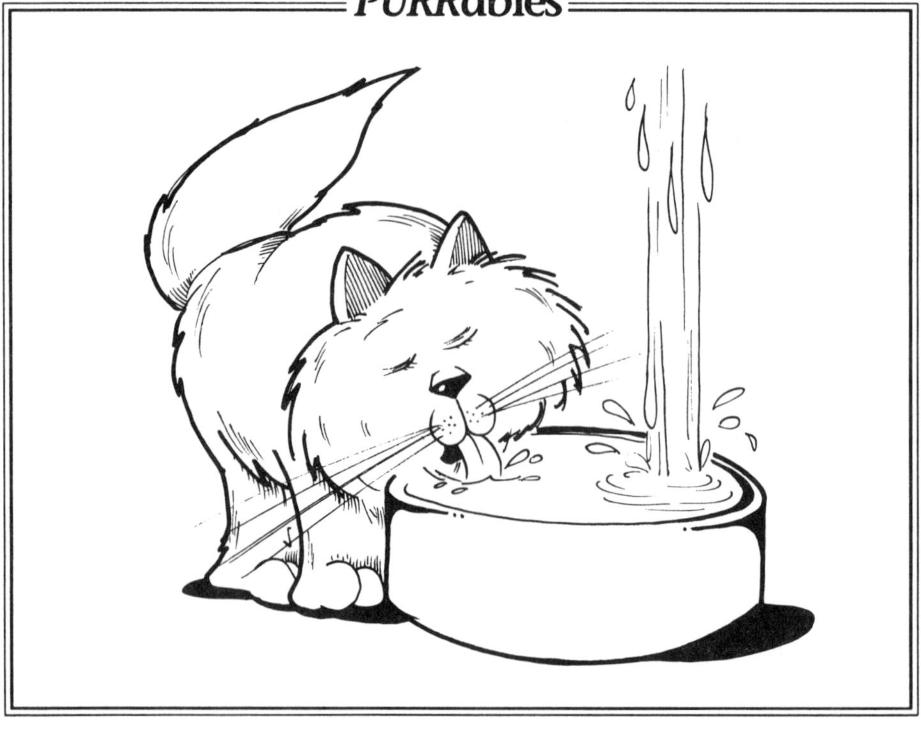

Reciprocating—

I go home from the animal hospital and wait, and the vet stands by and waits. It's like being in a taxi with the meter running. The longer it takes for Sir Purrcival to void, the more money flows from my bank account into the vet's pocket.

Totally unconcerned that he is slowly, inexorably pointing me in the direction of bankruptcy, Sir Purrcival is taking his jolly good time draining his bladder. Maybe he is evening the score on some feline grudge he harbors against me. Maybe he likes the attention he is getting in the emergency ward. Maybe it boosts his ego to know the vet is commanding double the current rate for overtime. Whatever the reason, Purrcival holds out for quite a few hours.

The vet finally assures us that Purrcival's bladder is flushed empty of sediment and we can pick up our patient. If I give him lots of water to drink, his drain shouldn't clog again. But if it does, I am to phone the vet. In other words, if I prime Purrcival's pump, I can be reasonably certain of avoiding bankruptcy. So far, so good. I am keeping his water dish filled to the brim, and Purrcival's plumbing remains fully operational.

One who gives water will get water. —Proverbs11:25

Enthralled—

On a bright day, a sunbeam streaming through the window at lunch time often reflects off our son's wristwatch, creating a moving spot of light on the floor.

The tomcat goes berserk. That roving spotlight is the most elusive goal the tomcat has ever sought, and he is bound to capture it. Knowing Sir Purrcival can do with the exercise, our son deliberately moves his arm in random directions. Now the spotlight is racing across the floor, now sweeping up the side of the frig, now rushing down the hall, now circling the room, and Sir Purrcival is in hot *purr*suit. I have never seen him get such a workout.

Long after our son has gone back to school, Purrcival lies panting on a chair, his feline brow wrinkled in bewilderment. The desire to capture that spotlight figures prominently in his mind. Why it always eludes his grasp is puzzling indeed. *Is a mouse not a moving target? Then this moving target must surely be a mouse.* Too mesmerized to stop and distinguish between the two, he is foolishly expending all of his energy in pursuing a mere reflection of success instead of devoting his time and efforts on the real thing.

Those who follow worthless pursuits have no sense. —Proverbs 12:11

PURRables

Combative—

Every evening when friend hubby and I settled down before the TV to listen to the latest developments in the Persian Gulf War, we would notice Purrcival turn into a feline version of a scud missile. Launched from some secret site where he had been hiding, he would go streaking down the hallway toward phantom targets, scaring us half to death.

Trying to restore some measure of peace to the household, I tried to stop him more than once, only to discover I don't make a very good Patriot interceptor.

My reflexes are not programmed fast enough.

When the history of Purrcival's unprovoked attacks come up for discussion at the vet's office, I wonder aloud whether cats pick up on our tension and then release it unexpectedly. The vet reminds me that hostile aggression is instinctive to all felines, hence their unpredictable behavior. He further advises that should Sir Purrcival initiate offensive action for no apparent reason, the best fire power I can employ is a loaded water pistol. That way neither one of us will get hurt.

Since several other experts in feline behavior concur with his advice, I march straight home to the old toy box and get myself well-armed.

By wise guidance you can wage your war and in abundance of counselors there is victory. —Proverbs 24:6

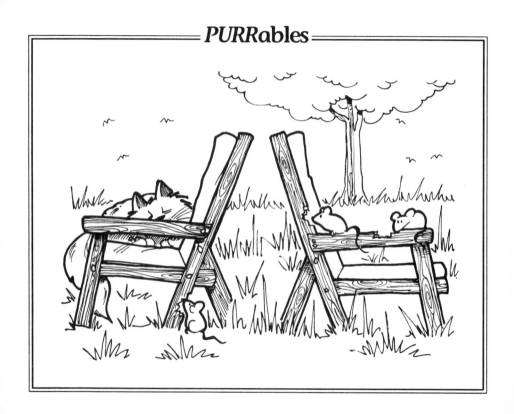

Unambitious—

Bulldozers at a new housing site rumble and growl as they uproot Sir Purrcival's favorite hunting grounds. He sits on the back step pondering this latest development, dark thoughts reflected in eyes as big as onyx saucers.

You'd think these humans would be more careful about the balance of nature. Here I am, a perfectly good tomcat ready and able to keep any pesky varmints under control and provide myself a good living at the same time. But no, progress is moving in and forcing me to the point of ruination. Now I'll have to go a whole block farther to mouse.

Such an alternative is not that appealing to Sir Purrcival. He'll have to get up earlier and come home later. Who knows? Maybe the mice at the new location will be trickier to catch and he'll have to brush up on his skills. It's been a long time since he *really* had to apply himself to the task at hand; he decides the returns are not worth the effort. Who cares if the neighborhood is overrun with pests and ends up in ruins?

Having thus justified his decision, he yawns, stretches and strolls leisurely over to his dish. It's easier to live on handouts.

One who is slack in work is close kin to a vandal. —Proverbs 18:9

Composed—

While doing spring cleaning, I decide to move the bed on which Sir Purrcival is sound asleep. For all he knows, the tremors could be caused by an earthquake measuring nine on the Richter scale. But he just opens one eye, secures his claws in the bedspread, and goes back to sleep.

A scant two hours later come the aftershocks—I move the bed back the other way. It still never occurs to him that he might be situated right over the San Andreas fault. Totally ignoring my evacuation orders, he yawns, stretches, and drifts back to sleep.

Nor is he greatly alarmed when the tornado-like sounds of the vacuum cleaner follow hard on the heels of the earthquake. I suppose he figures that if he has survived one natural disaster, he can outlive another.

The tomcat never has been one to panic over a little dust storm—much less go berserk in a whirlwind of spring cleaning. As I lie awake, suffering from sore muscles brought on by sudden and foolish exertion, I have to acknowledge that Sir Purrcival's balanced approach to life is certainly more conducive to a peaceful night's rest than my own hectic agenda.

Keep sound wisdom and prudence, . . . when you lie down, your sleep will be sweet. —Proverbs 3:21, 24

PURRables

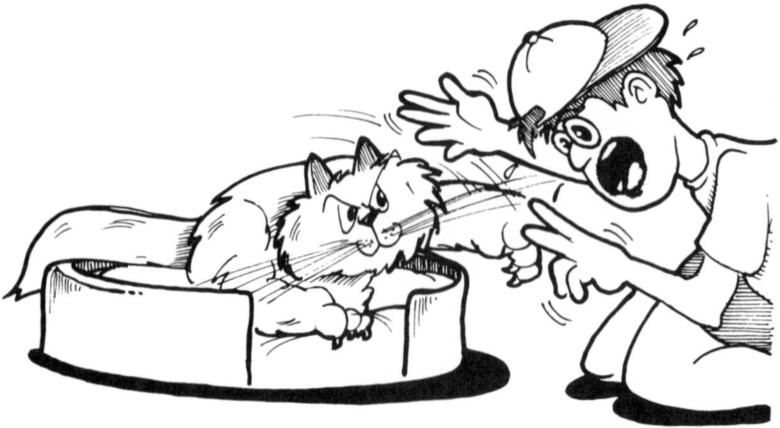

Reproving—

Contrary to popular belief, the west was not entirely won by settlers who carried muskets in their hands, but by little girls who smuggled kittens in their pockets. Those kittens grew up to be as much in demand as fine old Canadian mousers. Noble ancestors of Sir Purrcival, who now commands respect if only for his historic links to the past.

But he also earns his keep.

On occasion, I have hosted one of those undisciplined, obnoxious little brats whose mother thinks Johnny can do no wrong. Invariably, the mother is a strong advocate of permissive "training," which means that, while she passively files her nails, her child can tear my house apart—along with everything in it.

But in the course of his rampage, let Johnny latch onto my surly old tomcat. With one swipe of his outstretched claws, Sir Purrcival can exert more training than Johnny has ever received in all his five years. For the first time in his life, Johnny has learned that abusing another's property can bring painful consequences.

The experience may well curb the inclinations of a future vandal. At the very least, it preserves my premises intact for the remainder of Johnny's visit. For that reason alone, Sir Purrcival is worth his weight in cat food.

There is severe discipline for one who forsakes the way. —Proverbs 15:10

PURRables

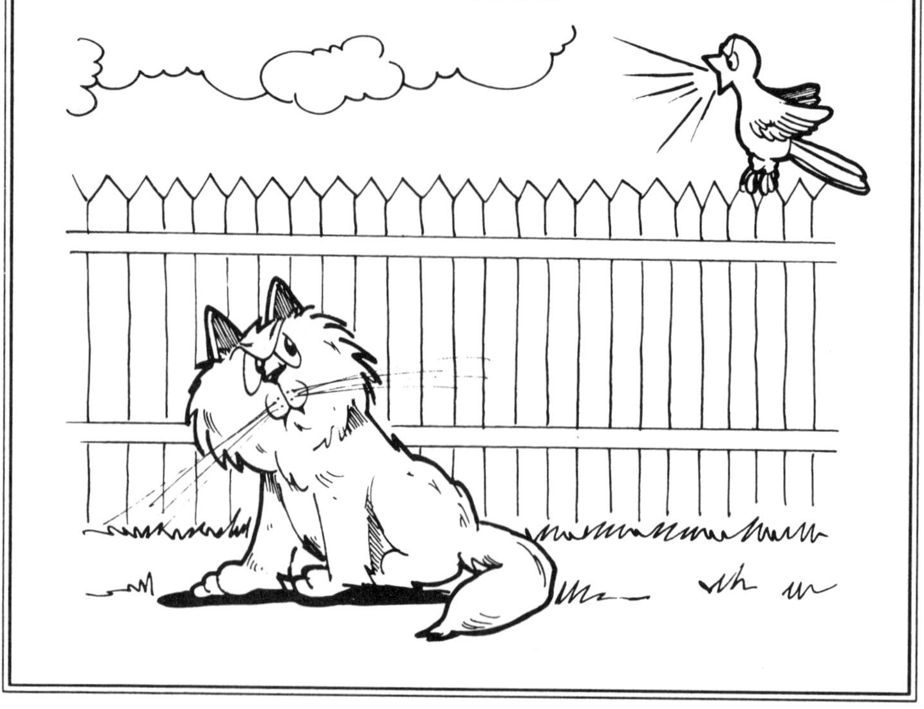

Insulted—

I have been known to banish Sir Purrcival to the basement for killing birds. But this summer he has enjoyed relative freedom, thanks to an unlikely source. A robin is nesting in the back yard. Every time she sees Sir Purrcival out stalking any member of the winged species, she sits bravely on the fence and broadcasts reprimands in bird language so emphatic it frustrates Sir Purrcival's plans. He would be loathe to admit she is a friend; but her admonitions have nevertheless spared him countless hours confined to the basement.

As if being pricked in the conscience by that bird is not painful enough. Sir Purrcival is now expected to get all dolled up in his collar and go to the vet's for a rabies shot. Apparently, that little black and white kitty with the strong perfume has created quite a panic among the people population. Sir Purrcival never can figure why he should get a needle when it's the skunk who gets sick. It's the ultimate indignity to be stabbed in the flank by a "friendly" vet and then carted home again.

Well meant are the wounds a friend inflicts. —Proverbs 27:6

Illustrations—Artwork
Copyright ©1993 by Starburst, Inc.
All rights reserved.

Resigned—

For Sir Purrcival, as for most of us, life is rather routine. Every morning he goes out to take his customary stroll around the yard, and then comes inside to see if anything of interest is going on.

He checks out the bedroom first. *Nope, the bed is already made. Shucks! He likes to pounce around when I'm flapping the sheets, capturing phantom intruders and generally making a nuisance of himself.*

Well then, he'll try the sewing room. There's nothing like lounging on a warm ironing board between pressings. If he *really* wants some attention, going to sleep on the scissors will bring production to a halt every time. He just has to act *very innocent while the seamstress searches for her shears. Alas! Nobody is sewing today.*

Maybe he should try the kitchen. If he can trip the cook and capture a windfall of sausages, it will make his day. But nothing looks very promising now. He'll have to wait until mealtime.

If all else fails, he can always curl up in the big easy chair and have a long overdue catnap, not at all *purr*turbed that life is mostly what you make it, or what it makes of you.

The perverse get what their ways deserve, and the good, what their deeds deserve. —Proverbs 14:14

Books by Starburst Publishers
(Partial listing—full list available on request)

A Woman's Guide To Spiritual Power
—Nancy L. Dorner

Subtitled: *Through Scriptural Prayer*. Do your prayers seem to go "against a brick wall?" Does God sometimes seem far away or non-existent? If your answer is "Yes," *You* are not alone. Prayer must be the cornerstone of your relationship to God. "This book is a powerful tool for anyone who is serious about prayer and discipleship."—Florence Littauer

(trade paper) ISBN 0914984470 **$9.95**

Get Rich Slowly . . . But Surely!
—Randy L. Thurman

The only get-rich-quick guide you'll ever need. Achieving financial independence is important to young and old. Anyone who wants to be financially free will discover the way to financial independence easier by applying these long-term, time-tested principles. This book can be read in one sitting!

(trade paper) ISBN 0914984365 **$7.95**

Stay Well Without Going Broke
—Gulling, Renner & Vargas

Provides a blueprint for how health care consumers can take more responsibility for monitoring their own health and the cost of its care—a crucial cornerstone of the health care reform movement today. Contains inside information from doctors, pharmacists and hospital personnel on how to get cost-effective care without sacrificing quality. Offers legal strategies to protect your heirs when illness is terminal.

(hard cover) ISBN 0914984527 **$22.95**

Purchasing Information: Listed books are available from your favorite Bookstore, either from current stock or special order. To assist bookstore in locating your selection be sure to give title, author, and ISBN #. If unable to purchase from the bookstore you may order direct from STARBURST PUBLISHERS. When ordering enclose full payment plus $2.50* for shipping and handling ($3.00* if Canada or Overseas). Payment in US Funds only. Please allow two to three weeks minimum (longer overseas) for delivery. Make checks payable to and mail to STARBURST PUBLISHERS, P.O. Box 4123, LANCASTER, PA 17604. **Prices subject to change without notice**. Catalog available upon request.